NOMADS
OF SOUTH PERSIA

Nomads
of South Persia

The Basseri Tribe
of the Khamseh Confederacy

FREDRIK BARTH

WAVELAND

PRESS, INC.

Prospect Heights, Illinois

For information about this book, write or call:

Waveland Press, Inc.
P.O. Box 400
Prospect Heights, Illinois 60070
(847) 634-0081

Copyright © 1961 by Fredrik Barth
Published under arrangement with Scandinavian University Press,
Oslo, Norway.
1986 reissued by Waveland Press, Inc.

ISBN 0-88133-207-0

Printed in the United States of America

12 11 10 9 8

CONTENTS

LIST OF FIGURES

FOREWORD

The following study is based on material collected in the field in Iran in the period December 1957 to July 1958 while I was engaged in research on nomads and the problems of sedentarization under the Arid Zone Major Project of UNESCO. Through the courtesy of H. E. Mr. Ala, the Court Minister, special permission was obtained from the Iranian Chief of Staff to enable me to spend the period 1/3 to 1/6 1958 among the Basseri nomads. Before and after that period, briefer visits were made to sedentary communities and other tribes in the province of Fars.

My thanks are first and foremost due to Mr. Hassan Ali Zarghami, the former chief of the Basseri, who gave me his full support in my studies and who made all possible arrangements for my comfort; to Ghulam Islami and his family, who received me into their tent and made me feel welcome as a member of their household throughout the duration of my stay; and to Ali Dad Zare, who served me with competence and patience as field assistant. I also recognize a debt to many other persons who have facilitated this work: to members of the Basseri tribe and particularly of the Darbar camp, and to friends and officials in Iran and elsewhere. In particular I want to mention Professor Morgenstierne of the University of Oslo, with whom I read Persian.

There are few previous studies in the literature on any of the nomadic groups in the Middle East, and none on the Khamseh. I have therefore seen it as an important duty in the following study to put down as much as possible of what I was able to observe of the society and culture of the Basseri. But this end is not best served by a mere compilation of a body of such observations — rather, I have tried through an analysis to "understand" or interrelate as many of these facts as possible.

The following pages present this analysis in terms of a general ecologic viewpoint. As the work grew, so did my realization of the extent to which most of the data are interconnected in terms of the possibilities and restrictions implied in a pastoral adaptation in the South Persian environment. Most of the following chapters describe different aspects of this adaptation. Starting with the elementary units of tents, or households, a description is given of the progressively larger units of herding groups, camps, the whole tribe and its major divisions, and the unifying political structure of the tribe and the confederacy. Throughout this description I try to reduce the different organizational forms to the basic processes by which they are maintained, and adapted to their environment. The subsequent chapters analyse more specifically some of these processes as they serve to maintain the tribe as an organized and persisting unit in relation to the outside, mainly within the systems of political relations, economic transactions, and demographics. The final chapter draws together the results of this analysis, and tries to apply the resulting model of Basseri organization to a comparative discussion of some features of nomadic organization in the South Persian area.

There are a number of reasons why some kind of ecologic orientation is attractive in the analysis of the Basseri data. Some of these may be subjective and reflect the personal needs of the investigator, rather than the analytic requirements of the material. Perhaps this framework of analysis is particularly attractive because some features of nomadic life are so striking to any member of a sedentary society. The drama of herding and migration; the idleness of a pastoral existence, where the herds satisfy the basic needs of man, and most of one's labour is expended on travelling and maintaining a minimum of personal comfort, and hardly any of it is productive in any obvious sense; the freedom, or necessity, of movement through a vast, barren and beautiful landscape — all these things assume a growing aesthetic and moral importance as one participates in nomadic life, and seem to call for an explanation in terms of the specific circumstances which have brought them forth. Perhaps also the poverty of ceremonial, and the eclectic modernism of the attitude of the Basseri, encourage an approach which relates cultural forms to natural circumstances, rather than to arbitrary premises. At all events, a great number of features of Basseri life and organization make sense and hang together as adaptations to a pastoral existence, and in terms of their implications for other aspects of the economic, social, and political life of the pastoral nomad population of Fars.

Oslo, October 1959.

F. B.

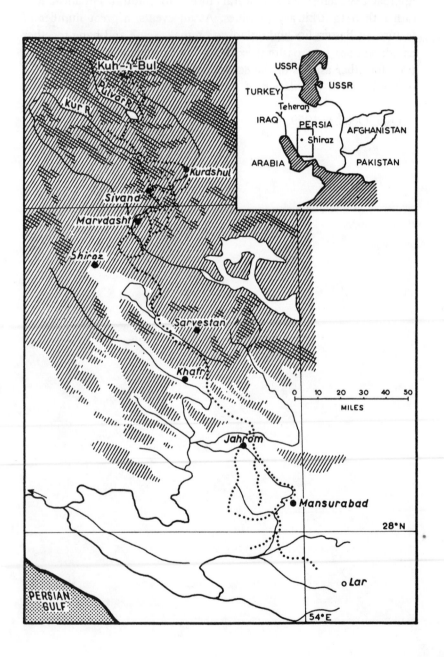

Chapter I

HISTORY, ECOLOGY AND ECONOMY

The Basseri are a tribe of tent-dwelling pastoral nomads who migrate in the arid steppes and mountains south, east and north of Shiraz in Fars province, South Persia. The area which they customarily inhabit is a strip of land, approximately 300 miles long and 20-50 miles wide, running in a fairly straight north-south line from the slopes of the mountain of Kuh-i-Bul to the coastal hills west of Lar. In this strip the tribe travels fairly compactly and according to a set schedule, so the main body of the population is at no time dispersed over more than a fraction of the route; perhaps something like a 50-mile stretch, or 2,000 square miles.

Fars Province is an area of great ethnic complexity and admixture, and tribal units are best defined by political, rather than ethnic or geographical criteria. In these terms the Basseri are a clearly delimited group, recognizing the authority of one supreme chief, and treated as a unit for administrative purposes by the Iranian authorities. The Basseri have furthermore in recent history been associated with some other tribes in the larger Khamseh confederacy; but this grouping has today lost most of its political and social meaning.

The total population of the Basseri probably fluctuates between 2,000 and 3,000 tents, depending on the changing fortunes of their chiefs as political leaders, and on the circumstances of South Persian nomadism in general. Today it is estimated at nearly 3,000 tents, or roughly 16,000 inhabitants.

The Basseri tribe is Persian-speaking, using a dialect very close to the urban Persian of Shiraz town; and most tribesmen know only that language, while some are bilingual in Persian and Turkish and

1

a few in Persian and Arabic. All these three language communities are represented among their neighbours. Adjoining them in most of their route is the smaller Kurdshuli tribe, speaking the Luri dialect of Persian and politically connected with the Qashqai confederacy. Politically dependent on the Basseri are the remnants of the Turkish-speaking Nafar tribe. The territories to the east are mostly occupied by various Arab tribes, some still Arabic-speaking and some Persian of the same dialect as the Basseri. Other adjoining areas to the east are dominated by the now largely sedentary Baharlu Turkish-speaking tribe. All these eastern tribes were associated with the Basseri in the Khamseh confederacy. The opposing Qashqai confederacy dominates the territories adjoining the Basseri on the west, represented by various branches of which the Shishbeluki are among the most important. These tribes are Turkish-speaking.

In addition to the Basseri population proper, various other groups are found that regard themselves as directly derived from the Basseri, while other groups claim a common or collateral ancestry. In most of the villages of the regions through which the Basseri migrate, and in many other villages and towns of the province, including Shiraz, is a considerable sedentary population of Basseri origin. Some of these are recent settlers — many from the time of Reza Shah's enforced settlement in the 30's and some even later — while others are third or fourth generation. In some of the villages of the north, notably in the Chahardonge area, the whole population regards itself as a settled section of the tribe, while in other places the settlers are dispersed as individuals or in small family groups.

Several other nomad groups also recognize a genetic connection with the Basseri. In the Isfahan area, mostly under the rule of the Dareshuri Turkish chiefs, are a number of Basseri who defected from the main body about 100 years ago and now winter in the Yazd-Isfahan plain and spend the summer near Semirun (Yazd-e-Khast). In north-west Fars a tribe generally known as the Bugard-Basseri migrates in a tract of land along the Qashqai-Boir Ahmed border. Finally, on the desert fringe east of Teheran, around Semnan, there is reported a considerable tribal population calling themselves Basseri, who are known and recognized as a collateral group by the Basseri of Fars.

The sparse historical traditions of the tribe are mainly connected

2

with sectional history (pp. 52 ff.), or with the political and heroic exploits of recent chiefs (pp. 72 ff.). Of the tribe as a whole little is recounted, beyond the assertion that the Basseri have always occupied their present lands and were created from its dust — assertions contradicted by the particular traditions of the various sections.

Early Western travellers prove poor sources on the nomad tribes of Persia; but at least tribal names and sections are frequently given. The Basseri are variously described as Arab and Persian, as largely settled and completely nomadic. An early reference to them is found in Morier (1837: 232), based on materials collected in 1814-15. One would guess from the paucity of information on the tribe that it was relatively small and unimportant; overlordship over the tribe had, according to Persian historical compilations, been entrusted to the Arab chiefs in Safavid times (Lambton 1953: 159). According to the Ghavams, leaders of the Khamseh, the confederacy was formed about 90-100 years ago by the FaFaFa of the present Ghavam. In the beginning the Turk tribes of Baharlu and Aynarlu were predominant among the Khamseh, and the Basseri grew in importance only later. Most Basseri agree that the tribe has experienced a considerable growth in numbers and power during the last three generations.

During the enforced settlement in the reign of Reza Shah only a small fraction of the Basseri were able to continue their nomadic habit, and most were sedentary for some years, suffering a considerable loss of flocks and people. On Reza Shah's abdication in 1941 migratory life was resumed by most of the tribesmen. The sections and camp-groups of the tribe were re-formed and the Basseri experienced a considerable period of revival. At present, however, the nomads are under external pressure to become sedentary, and the nomad population is doubtless on the decline.

The habitat of the Basseri tribe lies in the hot and arid zone around latitude 30° N bordering on the Persian Gulf. It spans a considerable ecologic range from south to north, ranging from low-lying salty and torrid deserts around Lar at elevations of 2,000 to 3,000 ft. to high mountains in the north, culminating in the Kuh-i-Bul at 13,000 ft. Precipitation is uniformly low, around 10″, but falls mainly in the winter and then as snow in the higher regions, so a considerable amount is conserved for the shorter growing season in that area. This permits considerable vegetation and occasional stands of forest to

3

develop in the mountains. In the southern lowlands, on the other hand, very rapid run-off and a complete summer drought limits vegetation, apart from the hardiest desert scrubs, to a temporary grass cover in the rainy season of winter and early spring.

Agriculture offers the main subsistence of the population in the area, though not of the Basseri. It is under these conditions almost completely dependent on artificial irrigation. Water is drawn by channels from natural rivers and streams in the area, or, by the help of various contraptions, raised by animal traction from wells, particularly by oxen and horses. Finally, complex nets of *qanats* are constructed — series of wells connected by subterranean aqueducts, whereby the groundwater of higher areas is brought out to the surface in lower parts of the valleys.

The cultivated areas, and settled populations, are found mostly in the middle zone around the elevation of Shiraz (5,000 ft. altitude), and also, somewhat more sparsely, as more or less artificial oases in the south. Settlement in the highest zones of the north is most recent, and still very sparse.

The pastoral economy of the Basseri depends on the utilization of extensive pastures. These pastures are markedly seasonal in their occurrence. In the strip of land utilized by the Basseri different areas succeed each other in providing the necessary grazing for the flocks. While snow covers the mountains in the north, extensive though rather poor pastures are available throughout the winter in the south. In spring the pastures are plentiful and good in the areas of low and middle altitude; but they progressively dry up, starting in early March in the far south. Usable pastures are found in the summer in areas above c. 6,000 ft; though the grasses may dry during the latter part of the summer, the animals can subsist on the withered straw, supplemented by various kinds of brush and thistles. The autumn season is generally poor throughout, but then the harvested fields with their stubble become available for pasturage. In fact most landowners encourage the nomads to graze their flocks on harvested and fallow fields, since the value of the natural manure is recognized.

The organization of the Basseri migrations, and the wider implications of this pattern, have been discussed elsewhere (Barth 1960). An understanding of the South Persian migration and land use pattern

4

is facilitated by the native concept of the *il-rah,* the "tribal road". Each of the major tribes of Fars has its traditional route which it travels in its seasonal migrations. It also has its traditional schedule of departures and duration of occupations of the different localities; and the combined route and schedule which describes the locations of the tribe at different times in the yearly cycle constitutes the *il-rah* of that tribe. Such an *il-rah* is regarded by the tribesmen as the *property* of their tribe, and their rights to pass on roads and over uncultivated lands, to draw water everywhere except from private wells, and to pasture their flocks outside the cultivated fields are recognized by the local population and the authorities. The *route* of an *il-rah* is determined by the available passes and routes of communication, and by the available pastures and water, while the *schedule* depends on the maturation of different pastures, and the movements of other tribes. It thus follows that the rights claimed to an *il-rah* do not imply exclusive rights to any locality throughout the year, and nothing prevents different tribes from utilizing the same localities at different times — a situation that is normal in the area, rather than exceptional.

The Basseri *il-rah* extends in the south to the area of winter dispersal south of Jahrom and west of Lar. During the rainy season camps are pitched on the mountain flanks or on the ridges themselves to avoid excessive mud and occasional flooding. In early spring the tribes move down into the mainly uncultivated valleys of that region, and progressively congregate on the Benarou-Mansurabad plain. The main migration commences at the spring equinox, the time of the Persian New Year. The route passes close by the market town of Jahrom, and northward over a series of ridges and passes separating a succession of large flat valleys. The main bottleneck, both for reasons of natural communication routes and because of the extensive areas of cultivation, is the Marvdasht plain, where the ruins of Persepolis are located. Here the Basseri pass in the end of April and beginning of May, crossing the Kur river by the Pul-e-Khan or Band-Amir bridges, or by ferries. In the same period, various Arab and Qashqai tribes are also funnelled through this area.

Continuing northward, the Basseri separate and follow a number of alternative routes, some sections lingering to utilize the spring pastures in the adjoining higher mountain ranges, others making

5

a detour to the east to pass through some villages recently acquired by the Basseri chief. The migration then continues into the uppermost Kur valley, where some sections remain, while most of the tribe pushes on to the Kuh-i-Bul area, where they arrive in June.

While camp is moved on most days during this migration, the population becomes more stationary in the summer, camping for longer periods and moving only locally. The first camps commence the return journey in the end of August, to spend some weeks in the Marvdasht valley grazing their flocks on the stubble and earning cash by labour; most go in the course of September. As the pastures are usually poor the tribe travels rapidly with few or no stops, and reaches the south in the course of 40—50 days, by the same route as the spring journey. During winter, as in the summer, migrations are local and short and camp is broken only infrequently.

The Basseri keep a variety of domesticated animals. Of far the greatest economic importance are *sheep* and *goats,* the products of which provide the main subsistence. Other domesticated animals are the *donkey* for transport and riding (mainly by women and children), the *horse* for riding only (predominantly by men), the *camel* for heavy transport and wool, and the *dog* as watchdog in camp. Poultry are sometimes kept as a source of meat, never for eggs. Cattle are lacking, reportedly because of the length of the Basseri migrations and the rocky nature of the terrain in some of the Basseri areas.

There are several common strains of sheep in Fars, of different productivity and resistance. Of these the nomad strain tends to be larger and more productive. But its resistance to extremes of temperature, particularly to frost, is less than that of the sheep found in the mountain villages, and its tolerance to heat and parched fodder and drought is less than that of the strains found in the south. It has thus been the experience of nomads who become sedentary, and of occasional sedentary buyers of nomad livestock, that 70-80 % of the animals die if they are kept throughout the year in the northern or southern areas. The migratory cycle is thus necessary to maintain the health of the nomads' herds, quite apart from their requirements for pastures.

Sheep and goats are generally herded together, with flocks of up to 300-400 to one shepherd unassisted by dogs. About one ram is required for every five ewes to ensure maximal fertility in the flock,

6

whereas in the case of goats the capacity of a single male appears to be much greater. The natural rutting seasons are three, falling roughly in June, August/September, and October; and the ewes consequently throw their lambs in November, January/February, or March. Some sections of the tribe (e. g. the Il-e-Khas) who winter further north in the zone of middle altitude separate the rams and the ewes in the August/September rutting period to prevent early lambing.

Lambs and kids are usually herded separately from the adults, and those born during the long migrations are transported strapped on top of the nomads' belongings on donkeys and camels for the first couple of weeks. A simple device to prevent suckling, a small stick through the lamb's mouth which presses down the tongue and is held in place by strings leading back behind the head, is used to protect the milk of the ewes when lambs and kids travel with the main herd. Early weaning is achieved by placing the lamb temporarily in a different flock from that of its mother.

The animals have a high rate of fertility, with moderately frequent twinning and occasionally two births a year. However, the herds are also subject to irregular losses by disaster and pest; mainly heavy frosts at the time of lambing, and foot-and-mouth disease and other contagious animal diseases. In bad years, the herds may suffer average losses of as much as 50 %. Contrary to general reports, the main migrations are not in themselves the cause of particular losses of livestock, by accident or otherwise.

The products derived from sheep and goats are milk, meat, wool and hides, while of the camel only the wool is used. These products are variously obtained and processed, and are consumed directly, stored and consumed, or traded.

Milk and its products are most important. Sheep's and goats' milk are mixed during milking. Milk is never consumed fresh, but immediately heated slightly above body temperature, and started off by a spoonful of sour milk or the stomach extract of a lamb; it then rapidly turns into sour milk or junket respectively. Cheese is made from the junket; it is frequently aged but may also be consumed fresh. Cheese production is rarely attempted in periods of daily migrations, and the best cheese is supposed to be made in the relatively stationary period of summer residence.

Sour milk *(mast)* is a staple food, and particularly in the period

7

of maximal production in the spring it is also processed for storage. By simple pressing in a gauze-like bag the curds may be separated from the sour whey; these curds are then rolled into walnut-sized balls and dried in the sun *(kashk)* for storage till winter. The whey is usually discarded or fed to the dogs; the Il-e-Khas are unusual, and frequently ridiculed, for saving it and producing by evaporation a solid residue called *qara ghorut,* analogous to Scandinavian "goat cheese".

Sour milk may also be churned, or actually rocked, in a goat skin *(mashk)* suspended from a tripod, to produce butter and buttermilk *(dogh).* The latter is drunk directly, the former is eaten fresh, or clarified and stored for later consumption or for sale.

Most male and many female lambs and kids are slaughtered for meat; this is eaten fresh and never smoked, salted or dried. The hides of slaughtered animals are valuable; lambskins bring a fair price at market, and the hides of adults are plucked and turned inside out, and used as storage bags for water, sour milk and buttermilk. The skins of kids, being without commercial value and rather small and weak, are utilized as containers for butter etc.

Wool is the third animal product of importance. Lamb's wool is made into felt, and sheep's wool and camel-hair are sold, or spun and used in weaving and rope-making. Goat-hair is spun and woven.

In the further processing of some of these raw products, certain skills and crafts are required. Though the nomads depend to a remarkable extent on the work of craftsmen in the towns, and on industrial products, they are also dependent on their own devices in the production of some essential forms of equipment.

Most important among these crafts are spinning and weaving. All locally used wool and hair is spun by hand on spindlewhorls of their own or Gypsy (cf. pp. 91-93) production — an activity which consumes a great amount of the leisure time of women. All saddlebags, packbags and sacks used in packing the belongings of the nomads are woven by the women from this thread, as are the rugs used for sleeping. Carpets are also tied, as are the outer surfaces of the finest pack- and saddle-bags. Furthermore, the characteristic black tents consist of square tentcloths of woven goat-hair — this cloth has remarkable water-repellent and heat-retaining properties when moist, while when it is dry, i. e. in the summer season, it insulates against radiation heat and permits free circulation of air. All weaving and carpet-tying is done on a horizontal loom, the simplest with merely a movable pole to change the sheds. None of these often very attractive articles are produced by the Basseri for sale.

Otherwise, simple utilitarian objects of wood such as tent poles and pegs, wooden hooks and loops bent over heat, and camels' pack saddles are produced by the nomads themselves. Ropes for the tents, and for securing pack loads and hobbling animals are twined with 3-8 strands. Some of the broader bands for securing loads are woven. Finally, various repairs on leather articles, such as the horses' bridles, are performed by the nomads, though there is no actual production of articles of tanned leather. Clothes for women are largely sewn by the women from bought materials, while male clothes are bought ready made.

Hunting and collecting are of little importance in the economy, though hunting of large game such as gazelle and mountain goat and sheep is the favourite sport of some of the men. In spring the women collect thistle-sprouts and certain other plants for salads or as vegetables, and at times are also able to locate colonies of truffles, which are boiled and eaten.

The normal diet of the Basseri includes a great bulk of agricultural produce, of which some tribesmen produce at least a part themselves. Cereal crops, particularly wheat, are planted on first arrival in the summer camp areas, and yield their produce before the time of departure; or locally resident villagers are paid to plant a crop before the nomads arrive, to be harvested by the latter. The agriculture which the nomads themselves perform is quite rough and highly eclectic; informants agreed that the practice is a recent trend of the last 10-15 years. Agricultural work in general is disliked and looked down upon, and most nomads hesitate to do any at all. The more fortunate, however, may own a bit of land somewhere along the migration route, most frequently in northern or southern areas, which they as landlords let out to villagers on tenancy contracts, and from which they may receive from 1/6 to 1/2 of the gross crop. Such absentee "landlords" do no agricultural work themselves, nor do they usually provide equipment or seed to their tenants.

A great number of the necessities of life are thus obtained by trade. Flour is the most important foodstuff, consumed as unleavened bread with every meal; and sugar, tea, dates, and fruits and vegetables are

9

also important. In the case of most Basseri, such products are entirely or predominantly obtained by trade. Materials for clothes, finished clothes and shoes, all glass, china and metal articles including all cooking utensils, and saddles and thongs are also purchased, as well as narcotics and countless luxury goods from jewelry to travelling radios. In return, the products brought to market are almost exclusively clarified butter, wool, lambskins, and occasional live stock.

Chapter II

DOMESTIC UNITS

The Basseri count their numbers and describe their camp groups and sections in terms of *tents* (sing.: *khune* = house). Each such tent is occupied by an independent household, typically consisting of an elementary family; and these households are the basic units of Basseri society. They are units of production and consumption; represented by their male head they hold rights over all movable property including flocks; and they can even on occasion act as independent units for political purposes.

The external sign of the existence of such a social unit is the tent. This is a square structure of cloth woven from goat-hair, supported along the sides and in the corners by tent poles, and in the case of the larger tents also along the central line by a row of T-shaped poles. The size of the tent varies according to the means of the family which resides in it; but it is typically about 6 by 4 m, and 2 m high, supported by 5 poles along the long side and 3 poles along the short side, and composed of 5 separate cloths: 4 for walls and one for roof. These cloths are fastened together by wooden pins when the tent is pitched. At the proper position for each tentpole is a wooden loop, attached to the roof cloth; the ropes are stretched from these loops and the notched ends of the tentpoles support the ropes adjoining the loop, rather than the tent cloth itself. The lower part of the wall is formed by reed mats which are loosely leaned against the tent cloth and poles.

When travelling, the Basseri frequently pitch a smaller tent with fewer poles, using the roof cloth also for one wall and thereby producing a roughly cubical structure. When the weather is mild, a short or even a long side of the tent is left open, frequently by laying the wall

11

cloth on top of the slanting tentropes; when the weather is cold the living space is closed in snugly by four full walls, and the tent is entered by a corner flap. Very occasionally in the summer when the tribe passes through openly forested areas, the tent may be dispensed with for a night and the households camp in the open under separate trees.

The living space within the tent is commonly organized in a standard pattern. Water and milk skins are placed along one side on a bed of stones or twigs; the belongings of the family are piled in a high wall towards the back, closing off a narrow private section in the very back of the tent. A shallow pit for the fire is placed close to the entrance. Though these arrangements are fairly stereotyped, they are dictated by purely practical considerations and are without ritual meaning.

This structure is the home of a small family group. In one camp group of 32 tents the average number of persons per tent was 5.7. The household is built around one elementary family of a man, his wife and their children, with the occasional addition of unmarried or widowed close relatives who would otherwise be alone in their tent, or the wife and children of a married son who is the only son, or the most recent son to be married. The different types of household in one camp group were distributed as follows:

Composition of households:

incomplete families:

widow(er) and Chi 3
single man and Mo 1

elementary families:
Hu, Wi and Chi 22

elementary families with additions:
Hu, Wi and Chi + HuMo 1
Hu, Wi and Chi + HuBr 2

polygynous families
Hu, 2 Wi and Chi 2

extended patrilineal families
Hu, Wi, Chi, SoWi, SoChi 1

Total	32

The household occupying a tent is a commensal and property-owning group. Though title to animals and some other valuable items of movable property may be vested in individual members of the household, the right to dispose of such is controlled by the head of the household, and the products of the animals owned by different members are not differentiated but used in the joint economy of the household.

In addition to the tent, the household, in order to exist, needs to dispose of all the equipment necessary to maintain the nomadic style of life — rugs and blankets for sleeping, pails and skins for milk, pots for cooking, and packbags to contain all the equipment during migrations, etc. Even between close relatives the lending and borrowing of such equipment is minimal.

The household depends for its subsistence on the animals owned by its members. These must as a minimum include sheep and goats as producers, donkeys to transport the belongings on the migrations, and a dog to guard the tent. All men also aspire to own a riding stallion, though less than half the household heads appear ever to achieve this goal; and wealthier persons with many belongings also need a few camels for transport.

Among the Basseri today each household has about 6-12 donkeys and on an average somewhat less than 100 adult sheep and goats. Every adult man has his distinctive sheep-mark, which by a combination of a brand on the sheep's face and notching or cutting of one ear or both endeavours to be unique. Brothers frequently maintain their father's brand when dividing the flock, but modify the earmarks. Yet there is no great emphasis on lineal continuity of brands, and men sometimes arbitrarily decide to change their brand. Though the herds may be large, adults have a remarkable ability to recognize individual animals; and the sheep-marks are used more as proof of the identity of lost sheep *vis-à-vis* outsiders than to distinguish the animals of different owners who camp together.

There is normally no loaning or harbouring of animals except for weaning purposes; each household keeps its flock concentrated. Occasionally, however, wealthy men may farm out a part of their flock to propertyless shepherds on a variety of contracts (cf. Lambton 1953: 351 ff.). These are, among the Basseri:

dandune contract: the shepherd pays 10-15 Tomans (1 Toman =

roughly 1 shilling) per animal per year, keeps all products, and at the expiration of the contract returns a flock of the same size and age composition as he originally received.

teraz contract: the shepherd pays approximately 2 kg clarified butter per animal for the three spring months, and keeps all other products. If one of the flock stops giving milk in less than 45 days, he may have it replaced; if an animal is lost through anything but the negligence of the shepherd, the owner carries the loss.

nimei or *nisfei* contract (for goats only): the shepherd pays 30 Tomans/year per goat and keeps all its products; after termination of the contract period, usually 3-5 years, he keeps one half of the herd as it stands, and returns the other half to the original owner.

Such contracts are most common in periods when the flocks of the Basseri are large.

Domestic organization. Within each tent there is a distribution of authority and considerable division of labour among the members of the household. But this follows a highly elastic pattern, and it is characteristic that few features of organization are socially imperative and common to all, while many features vary, and appear to reflect the composition of each household and the working capacities of its members.

All tents have a recognized head, who represents the household in all dealings with the formal officers of the tribe, and with villagers and other strangers. Where the household contains an elementary family, the head is universally the husband in that family, even when his widowed father or senior brother resides with the family. Where the tent is occupied by an incomplete family, the senior male is the head. Only where there are no adult male members of the household, or where they are temporarily absent, is a woman ever regarded as the head of a household; and in such cases she is usually represented for formal purposes by a relative.

However, with respect to decisions in the domestic and familial domain, men and women are more nearly equal, and the distribution of authority between spouses is a matter of individual adaptation. Thus decisions regarding the multitude of choices in the field of production and consumption (but not decisions about migration routes and camp sites), all matters of kinship and marriage and the training of children, and decisions that will greatly affect the family,

14

such as whether to change one's group membership, or become sedentary, these are all decisions that are shared by the spouses and to some extent by the other adult members of the household, and in which the wiser or more assertive person dominates, regardless of sex. The internal authority pattern of the Basseri is thus very similar to that of the urban Western family.

Labour is divided among household members by sex and age, but few tasks are rigidly allotted to only one sex or one age group. The various labour tasks may be grouped in three categories: domestic work, the daily cycle of migration, and tending and herding of animals.

Domestic tasks are mainly done by the women and girls — they prepare food, wash and mend clothes, spin and weave, while the men and boys provide wood and water. But this latter is also frequently done by girls and sometimes by poor women, while men frequently make tea, or roast meat, or wash their own clothes. Spinning and weaving are never done by men, and male villagers are often ridiculed by the nomads for pursuing these activities. Most repairs of equipment and tents, twining of ropes, etc. are done by men.

About 120 days out of the year, the average Basseri camp is struck and repitched at a new location; and these frequent migrations consume much time and labour and strongly affect the organization of the daily round. Activity starts well before daylight, when the sheep and goats, which have spent the night by the tent, depart in the care of a shepherd who is usually a boy or man, but may also be a girl. The tent is usually struck before sunrise, while the household members snatch odds and ends of left-over food and drink tea for breakfast. The donkeys, which have roamed freely during the night in a common herd, are retrieved by a boy or man of the camp. Packing and loading are done by all, usually in a habitual way but with no formal division of labour. The total process of breaking camp may take about 1½ hours.

Most family members ride on top of the loaded donkeys during the migration, while one — boy, man, girl, or occasionally woman — follows on foot and drives the beasts. Men who own horses usually ride these at the head of the caravan. They thus determine the route and decide on the place to camp — usually after roughly 3 hours of travel at a brisk pace. Tent sites are seized by the men, sometimes

15

with a certain amount of argument, and the donkey caravan disperses to these sites. All household members co-operate in unloading the beasts and pitching the tent, the men moving the heaviest pieces. The donkeys are let loose and driven off by a child, or several children, while a larger child is sent off for brush to make a fire for tea.

The sheep and goats arrive in camp at about noon; after these are milked the women prepare a meal. Various domestic tasks are performed in the afternoon: just before sunset the flock is milked again, and the evening meal is taken late, just before sleep.

The work of tending the animals consists mainly of herding and milking. The shepherd for the main flock is almost always a male; as he is occupied with the flock from c. 4 a.m. to 6 p.m. he cannot simultaneously serve as head of household and perform the male domestic tasks in the tent and during migration. Boys down to the age of 6 are therefore frequently used as shepherds, while married men only exceptionally do such work. The smaller and less wide-ranging flocks of lambs and kids are usually looked after by smaller children of both sexes; or they may be divided, the weaned ones accompanying the main herd, the unweaned ones tethered in the tent.

Milking is done by both sexes, but mostly by women. The animals are fairly easy to control and may be milked individually by a single person. But a simpler **and more** systematic arrangement is preferred, whereby the flock is driven by shepherding children into a spear-head formation and forced to pass through the narrow point at its apex, where they are held by the shepherd or another male, while being milked by two or more persons on either side of the shepherd. Thereby those who do the milking need not move their pails, and the milked animals pass through and roam off, separated from the unmilked animals.

Household economy: A picture of the resultant economy and standard of living of the average Basseri household may be formed and to some extent cross-checked by a little simple arithmetic. The average suggested above of somewhat less than 100 sheep/goats per tent is based on Basseri estimates and agreed with a few rough counts that I made of the flock associated with tent camps. Only very few herd owners have more than 200 sheep, while informants agreed that it was impossible to subsist on less than 60. To maintain a satisfactory

16

style of life it was generally considered that a man with normal family commitments requires about 100 sheep and goats — so at present a majority of the Basseri fall somewhat short of this ideal. However, the flocks in 1958 were still suffering from losses experienced during and after a very bad season in 1956-7, and were thus unusually small.

The market value of a mature female sheep was at the time of field-work c. 80 Tomans, so the average flock represented a capital asset of c. 7,000 T., (roughly £ 350 or $ 1,000). In a different context, I was able several times to discuss family budgets in detail. The consensus of opinion and data is that a normal household needs to buy goods for an average value exceeding 3,000 T., while a comfortable standard of living implies a consumption level of 5-6,000 Ts' worth of bought goods per year.

These requirements seem at first sight out of proportion to the productive capital of 8,000 T. corresponding to the ideal average of a flock of 100 head. However, an estimate of the income produced by a fertile ewe gives consistency to the picture. In 1958, its estimated value was:

From one ewe in one year:		
	wool	c. 20 T.
	clarified butter	c. 25 T.
	lamb: skin	c. 15 T.
	Sum	c. 60 T.

leaving lamb's meat, buttermilk, and curds to be consumed by the nomad and his family. This sum, formerly greater, has suffered a severe reduction with the collapse of prices on "Shirazi" lambskins, until recently bought for as much as 50 T. Yet allowing both for a 10 % population of rams and billygoats in the herd, and a 15 % per annum rate of replacement of stock, a flock of 100 head should give a total product per annum of more than 5,000 T. value at 1958 prices.

Estimates based on different kinds of data thus agree on an average net income from the sale of produce of 3-5,000 T., or roughly £ 200, per annum per household for the Basseri in 1958, together with a considerable production of foodstuffs consumed directly, such as milk, milk products, and meat. This confirms one's overwhelming subjective impression of a high standard of living among the Basseri nomads relative to most populations in the Middle East.

17

Household maintenance and replacement. The description so far has been static, and has not touched on the crucial problem of the continuation and replacement of household units as a process spanning the generations. These problems are particularly interesting among pastoral nomads, and may be discussed in terms of the concept of household "viability" used by Stenning (1958) in his article on the pastoral Fulani.

The household units of the Basseri are based on elementary families; and this means that after a new marriage, when the nucleus of a new family is established, this nucleus forms a new and independent household. A woman joins her husband upon marriage, and after a few nights in a separate small bridal tent lives with him and his natal family in their tent. But the young couple's period of residence there is usually brief and rarely extends beyond the birth of the first child; as soon as possible they establish themselves in a separate tent as a separate household. As such they form an independent economic unit, and to be viable as such they must possess the productive property and control the necessary labour force to pursue the pastoral nomadic activities described above. In the following I shall try to describe the standard Basseri arrangements whereby productive property in the form of herds and equipment, and additional labour force, are provided to secure the viability of newly established, or in other respects incomplete, elementary families.

Though the herd of a household is administered and utilized as a unit, individual members of the household may, as noted, hold separate title to the animals. It is therefore possible for a young person to build up some capital in flocks while he still lives in his parents' tent. In times of plenty fathers frequently give a few animals to their younger sons, partly to stimulate their interest in caring for the animals, partly to test their luck as herd owners. Boys whose fathers are very poor usually seek work as shepherds for others; and in return for such work they are given a few lambs every year, and with good luck can build up a small herd that way.

The main transfers, however, take place at the time of marriage. The various transactions at marriage will be analysed below; we are here concerned only with those that contribute directly to setting up the new household. The expense of this is carried by the groom's father, who provides a cash bride-price which the bride's father is expected in part to use to equip his daughter with rugs, blankets, and household utensils, while the women of both households may contribute labour to weave cloth for the new tent. A payment of sheep is also usually made, and it is expected that these will later be passed on by the bride's father to his son-in-law, though this is not always done.

These customs contribute to the setting up of the married couple in a separate tent; but they do not provide the new household with the necessary flocks. This is achieved by a practice explicitly regarded by the Basseri as anticipatory inheritance, whereby a son at marriage receives from his father's herd the arithmetic fraction which he would receive as an heir if his father were to die at that moment. In such divisions, the right of the "widow" to a small share is recognized; otherwise only agnatic heirs are considered, and close agnates eliminate all more distant agnates, while a man often reserves for himself a share equal to that he allots to each son.

For example, as a boy a certain Alamdar, one of 5 brothers, was given a flock of 60 one-year-old lambs and kids; but he had bad luck and nearly all the animals were lost, his father appropriating the few that were left. When he married, his father made the bride payments and then gave Alamdar 1/6 of his herd (there being 5 sons plus himself and his wife to share).

In another case, Barun, the eldest of 6 sons, was married. At the time his father had 145 sheep, 9 donkeys, and 3 horses. The bride payment asked was 20 sheep. His father, wanting to set up his son well, waived his own right to a share, allotted 5 sheep to his wife, leaving 20 sheep as the share for one son. Barun also received 3 donkeys (which, being forbidden as food, increase more rapidly than sheep) and 1 horse. Barun received no return from his father-in-law on the bride payment.

A few years later his brother was married. Meanwhile the father's flock had grown to 200, and the groom received 40 sheep as his share as one of 5 remaining sons. No adjustment was made because of this difference between the shares given the first and the second sons on their marriage. In fact Barun's flock had meanwhile grown to 50 sheep; but even had he been propertyless by then he would have had no right to a further share. In such divisions, bride payments are always made before the departing son is allotted his share, while payments received on girls are added to the father's estate at the time of receipt, and sons who have separated from him before that time have no rights in such payments, and no other remaining claims on their father's flocks.

On the death of the father, however, a certain estate remains to be allocated. If the old man was living with a married son, or even a married daughter, all household property is regarded as the property of the resident spouses, with possible adjustments made in the case of particularly valuable items such as rugs etc. If a household is dissolved by the death of its head, his heirs divide the property. In such cases, daughters who are married in their natal tribal section, or are present for other reasons at the time of their father's death, usually receive a share of his estate.

In addition to flocks and household property, some nomads also own land, or money in a bank. Such property is never passed on while the owner is alive, but is divided by his heirs on his death. Though the claim is usually made that Koranic inheritance rules are observed with respect to land and money, they are in practice usually side-stepped, and the estate appropriated by the agnatic heirs. In cases of conflict over inheritance, the tribal authorities usually defer to the decision of civil or religious courts, where the rights of a daughter to half the share of a son are upheld. To forestall daughters in their claims to a share of the land, male agnatic heirs frequently give them for a few years "gifts" of a reasonable fraction of the produce of such lands.

Through such practices, a marrying couple are provided with the property in animals and equipment which they require to set themselves up as an economically independent household unit. But to maintain themselves in this position they must perform the whole set of tasks connected with pastoral nomadic subsistence. This requires the co-operation of at the very least three persons: a male head of household who performs male tasks around the tent and connected with the migration, a woman to perform female domestic tasks, and a male shepherd. Only in a restricted phase of its development, while it contains adolescent children, can an elementary family be expected to contain this necessary personnel. The ideal, and in fact relatively common, situation is one where the husband and head of household remains close to the tent, and accompanies the caravan

20

on migration, while one or several sons serve as shepherd boys. Where the family alone does not contain this labour team, other arrangements must be made.

Such arrangements may be of several kinds. A shepherd or servant may be engaged; childless couples may adopt a brother's son or other close male agnate; while most households enter into small co-operative herding units to secure additional labour by sharing the burdens.

The relationship between a shepherd or servant and his master is based on an explicit economic contract, whereby the former is supplied with food and shelter, new clothes at Nowruz (Spring equinox, the Persian New Year), and a salary of no more than 40-50 T. per year. Such contracts are taken only by propertyless, usually unmarried men; only rarely is the relationship so stable and remunerative for the shepherd that he can establish a family of his own.

The partners in such contracts are rarely close kin; on the other hand there is considerable reluctance to engage a shepherd or servant who is an outsider, and even more so if he is a stranger, since it is necessary to place considerable trust in him, both with regard to his treatment of the animals, and his respect for the family and property of his master. He lives as a member of the household by which he is engaged, but generally eats separate from, or subsequent to, his master. The ambition of such servants and shepherds is to establish themselves with a family as a small independent herd owner; and this goal they not infrequently achieve after 10-15 years of work. Less than one household in ten has the means to employ outside labour in this way.

Occasionally when a marriage proves barren, the childless couple may adopt a close agnate of the husband, preferably his brother's son, as their own child. In such cases the boy is used as shepherd as a real son would have been, and ultimately inherits his foster-parents' estate to the exclusion of other heirs.

Both these devices serve to maintain the isolated, individual household as a viable unit by supplementing its labour pool from outside sources. This independence and self-sufficiency of the nomad household, whereby it can survive in economic relation with an external market but in complete isolation from all fellow nomads, is a very striking and fundamental feature of Basseri organization.

However, to facilitate the herding and tending of the flocks, Basseri

21

households usually unite in groups of 2-5 tents. These combine their flocks and entrust them to a single shepherd, and co-operate during milking time. As noted, a shepherd is readily able to control a herd of up to 400 head, and there is some feeling that very small herds are relatively more troublesome; while milking is made easier when numerous people combine to drive and control the herd.

The tents of such a herding unit are always pitched together, in a line or a crescent, with the herd spending the night beside them; and when the herd is driven in for milking, most of the members of the unit assist. But each woman, or, occasionally, man, milks only the animals belonging to her or his own household, and generally departs when they are all done, not waiting for the other members of the herding unit to complete their milking.

The relationship among members of a herding unit is contractual, and is always regarded as a partnership among equals. Household heads are free to establish the relation with anyone they wish inside their own tribal section. The division of labour between members is based on expediency, and the person or persons who serve as shepherds are in no way regarded as the servants of the others; rather, the work they do is regarded as a favour, and rewarded by gifts of lambs. At any time, a member of a herding unit may withdraw from that group and work alone, or join another unit; and through time the constellations of households in herding units change completely.

By joining a herding unit, households can persist without the full complement of personnel to make them viable as fully independent units. It is sufficient that *one* of the component members of a herding unit provides a shepherd; and smaller households are thus motivated by practical considerations to join households with a secure labour supply, while these are interested in increasing their income by serving as herders for others.

Such practical considerations, as well as friendship and enmity, and a belief in the good or bad herding luck of different persons, seem to dominate a man's decisions about which herding unit he joins. Thus when disagreements arise, or the compositions of households change, herding unit membership tends to change.

Considerations of nearness of kinship, on the other hand, seem to be irrelevant to the composition of herding units. While married sons initially tend to retain their flocks in the old herd, and thus stay in

22

the herding unit of their father, these bonds are freely broken at any time; and there are no apparent regularities in the kinship composition of the herding units of the camp with which I spent most of my time. These are illustrated in Fig. 10; and in every unit, persons have combined with distant relatives and non-kin in spite of the presence in camp of very close kin. The composition of herding units thus seems to be determined by considerations of the availability of labour, the sizes of herds, and the distribution of friendship and mutual trust.

In this chapter I have tried to describe the basic unit of Basseri social organization: the household occupying a tent, and the activities whereby this unit maintains itself and reproduces itself. The picture is one of relatively great independence and self-sufficiency, whereby many households are viable in complete isolation from other Basseri, though strongly dependent on an external market in sedentary and agricultural communities. For purposes of more efficient herding, however, these households combine in small herding units, the composition of which reflects practical expediency for herding purposes, rather than kinship or other basic principles of organization.

Chapter III

CAMPS

During two or three months of winter, an extreme dispersal is advan. tageous for the Basseri population, since the pastures on which they depend at that time are poor but extensive. In winter therefore, the groups of 2-5 tents associated in herding units make up local camps, separated by perhaps 3-4 km from the next group. At all other times of the year camps are larger, and usually number 10-40 tents. This group migrates as a unit, and its tents are pitched close together in a more or less standard pattern. In the summer there is a certain tendency to fragmentation, but camps still remain larger than single herding units, even if the tents are generally further apart.

These camps are in a very real sense the primary communities of nomadic Basseri society; they correspond to hamlets or small compact villages among sedentary peoples. The members of a camp make up a very clearly bounded social group; their relations to each other as continuing neighbours are relatively constant, while all other contacts are passing, ephemeral, and governed by chance. In the following I shall attempt to describe the composition of such camp groups among the Basseri, and analyse their internal structure and organization.

There is one point that deserves emphasis, and that offers the point of departure for the following analysis. Unlike a sedentary community, which persists unless the members abandon their house and land and depart, a camp community of nomads can only persist through continuous re-affirmation by all its members. Every day the members of the camp must agree in their decision on the vital question of whether to move on, or to stay camped, and if they move, by which route and how far they should move. These decisions are the very stuff of a pastoral nomad existence; they spell the difference between growth and prosperity of the herds, or loss and poverty. Every household head has an opinion, and the prosperity of his household is dependent on the wisdom of his decision. Yet a single disagreement on this question between members of the camp leads to fission of the camp as a group — by next evening they will be separated by perhaps 20 km of open steppe and by numerous other camps, and it will have become quite complicated to arrange for a reunion. The maintenance of a camp as a social unit thus requires the daily unanimous agreement by all members on economically vital questions.

Such agreement may be achieved in various ways, ranging from coercion by a powerful leader to mutual consent through compromise by all concerned. The composition of a camp will thus indirectly be determined by the available means whereby the movements of economically independent households can be controlled and co-ordinated. In a sense, recruitment to a camp group is not a once-and-for-all allocation by some basic criterion to a stable group, but a daily process dependent on the attainment of agreement within the group. Rather, therefore, than start my analysis by scrutinizing some existing camps, so as to discover hidden principles of kinship which underly their composition, I shall base my analysis on the processes whereby the unity of a camp may be maintained.

This task is simplified by the existence of a recognized leader in every camp, who represents the group for political and administrative purposes, and on whom this analysis can focus. Leaders of different camps may be of two kinds: headmen (sing.: *katkhoda*) formally recognized by the Basseri chief, and, where no headman resides in camp, informal leaders (sing.: *riz safid*, lit. "whitebeard") who by common consent are recognized to represent their camp in the same way as a headman does, but without the formal recognition of the Basseri chief and therefore technically under a headman in a different camp. The distinction between these two categories has broken down somewhat since the Iranian Army assumed administrative control over the tribe two years ago, because of the practice of the administering Colonel to elevate all camp leaders to the status of formally recognized headmen. This, however, has as yet had little effect on their position in their own camp.

A leader holds his camp together by exercising authority and/or by

26

his influence in establishing and formulating unanimous agreement within the camp on questions of migration and camp sites. The position of the leaders of camps may thus be analysed in terms of their sources of authority, grouped under the following headings: The required authority to dictate decisions may depend on (a) political power derived from the central chief, (b) economic or (c) military power within the camp. The weaker and more diffuse influence sufficient for the task of establishing and formulating general agreement may derive from additional sources generally subsumed under the heading of (d) kinship.

Relations to the chief. An analysis of the position of the Basseri chief is given later; in the present context it is sufficient to know that he is the head of a very strongly centralized political system and has immense authority over all members of the Basseri tribe. However, the system does not depend on any delegation of power from the chief to subordinates. The ordinary leaders of tent camps, being without any formal recognition by the chief, naturally cannot base their authority on his support. But even the headmen which he formally recognizes are not vested by him with any special coercive means. They transmit, on occasion, his orders to the camp in general, and then in a sense speak with all the authority which such an order carries; but when they exercise their discretion in their personal capacity as headmen, the chief is in no way committed to their decisions, and when consulted makes his own decision without reference to possible previous rulings by the headman. This lack of support from above, except in special cases when the chief consciously tries to change the political constellations within a group, is also revealed in questions of succession. The office of headman is usually inherited in male line, with some regard for seniority. However, the members of a headman's group insist on their right to appoint anyone of their number as the successor, and the chief is expected merely to assent to their choice. The tribesmen also claim that they may depose their headman at will, and in such cases the chief reportedly rarely supports the old incumbent. The chief himself expressed this principle from his own point of view, saying that it is most convenient to have the headman who is most acceptable to his own group, since he is able most readily to effect the commands of the chief regarding that group. In other words, the chief in his dealings through the headmen draws on the power

27

and influence which they have established already by other means, and does not delegate any of his own power to them. The prestations that flow from the chief to the headmen are mostly gifts of some economic and prestige value, such as riding-horses and, especially in the past, weapons. The headman is also in a politically convenient position since he can communicate much more freely with the chief than can ordinary tribesmen, and thus can bring up cases that are to his own advantage, and to some extent block or delay the discussion of matters detrimental to his own interests. None the less, the political power which a headman derives from the chief is very limited.

Economic power. Headmen are never among the smallest herd owners in their group, and incumbency in the status calls for certain moderate expenditures on hospitality and general appearance which exclude the poorest strata. But the economic position of a headman is subject to the same fluctuations as that of any other herd owner, and there is little correlation between great wealth and headmanship. I know clear examples of serious economic regression in the case of some headmen, and this does not appear to affect their position greatly. Informants claimed that where a popular headman is impoverished by a serious loss of animals over a long period, the members of his group may decide to reconstitute his herd by voluntary or percentile gifts of animals. As for the authority which may be derived from wealth, persons who do have great wealth in flocks seem to have few techniques whereby they can convert such economic superiority directly to political power. The big herd owner has greatly enhanced prestige, but he does not manipulate his wealth to gain political control over a larger group of dependent followers; thus, where parts of his flocks are sub-let (cf. pp. 13-14) to others, contracts are preferably established with persons in *other* camp groups, so as to spread the economic risks, rather than within the camp, to gain control over camp members. The power and influence of headmen can thus to only a very small extent derive from economic sources.

Military power. Dominance by headmen through force is similarly incompatible with the usual forms of Basseri organization. A headman has no access to such sources of power outside the camp group, and is not empowered by the chief with special privileges to utilize force. As pointed out, each tent is an autonomous unit under its head, who has direct political relations with the chief without reference to his headmen, and small groups of 2-5 tents in a herding unit are economically completely self-sufficient. The only source of force for a headman is thus within his own tent, and to some extent within his own herding unit — a very small base from which to attempt to tyrannize a whole camp. I do know of a few relevant cases, one where a headman has disproportionate influence because of the activities of his group of married and unmarried sons, feared as bandits and thieves; the other is in the same group, where five brothers and two paternal cousins were able to challenge their headman's authority in a conflict still not resolved when I left the tribe. These men were able to meet force with force because of their numbers, and because they were unmarried, and therefore less vulnerable to the threatened reprisals. These cases, however, were regarded by the tribesmen as unusual and deplorable; and few headmen or other camp leaders rely to any great extent on the use of force to maintain their position.

Kinship. There is thus no basis in the Basseri system of organization for the exercise of a strong commanding authority by headmen, and even less by informal leaders of camps. The camp leader is dependent on his ability to influence camp members, to guide and formulate public opinion in the group. The authority required for this activity is derived from sources within the camp, and the composition of persisting camps reflects these sources. They are: agnatic kinship in a ramifying descent system, and matrilateral and affinal relations. In the case of an established leader the personal esteem which accrues to him from his experience and proved ability is of course important; but this does not significantly affect the composition of the camp, and is irrelevant to the crucial question of succession to leadership. The structurally significant sources of camp leader authority appear to be only those two named. Each of these requires separate discussion.

In matters of succession the *agnatic* line is given prominence among the Basseri, as among other tribal people in the Middle East. We have seen how sons and subsidiarily collateral patrikinsmen are favoured in inheritance to the extent of usually excluding daughters from access to their legally rightful share. Where membership in formal groups is transmitted by descent, the line chosen is always the patriline — thus the son of a Basseri is regarded as Basseri even though his mother may be from another tribe or from a village, while a Basseri woman who marries outside the tribe transmits no rights in the tribe to her offspring. The importance of agnatic kin is reinforced by an ideology of respect and deference for Fa, FaFa, and FaBr, and solidarity of Br.s, and the ideal of solidarity is extended laterally to patrilateral cousins and beyond.

There is thus a continual process of formation of small patrilineal nuclei: groups of brothers held together by their joint rights in their father's flock before their marriage, and certain residual economic interests, as well as the ideal of solidarity, after their marriage. There is also a normative extension of this solidarity to agnatic collaterals. But the genealogical knowledge that is necessary to make such an extension effective is poorly developed. Only few men know their own pedigrees in any depth (though a few informants were able to name as many as 8-11 ascending generations), and the genealogical map of agnatic collaterals is even less generally known.[1] As a source of influence over camp members, agnatic kinship can thus be utilized by leaders only to a limited extent — while the acceptance of lineal authority from ascendants is strong, the strength of lateral solidarity is slight and may even be too weak to keep brothers together. More frequently it seems that references to agnatic kinship are used as formal justifications, by both parties, for the influence that accrues to leaders by virtue of other factors.

Patrilineal descent is also of prominent importance in succession to the formal office of headman. As noted above (p. 27), the chief must confirm succession and insists on his right to appoint any new headman he likes, while the tribesmen similarly claim the right to choose their own leader — again independently of the candidate's kinship position. But with strong lineal identification, and succession by the son to other of his father's formal statuses, the headman's son is by far the strongest pretender and the most convenient candidate for the compromising parties. In cases I know where the preceding headman was not the present incumbent's father or brother, reference to this fact was usually avoided. Patrilineal succession is thus the rule, usually with due regard to the relative seniority of the headman's sons in terms of age, and not, in cases of polygyny, with reference to the status of their mothers.

---

[1] The importance of descent groups in the wider political system is discussed below, pp. 50-70, where the details of some genealogies are given.

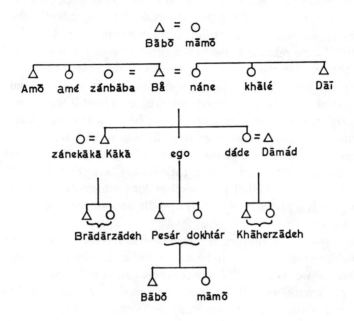

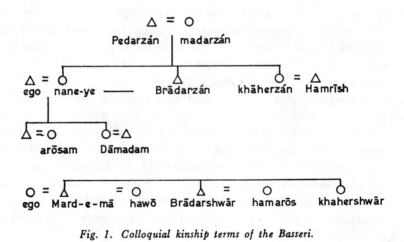

Fig. 1. Colloquial kinship terms of the Basseri.

31

While patrilineal kinship is used to conceptualize larger kin-based groups and is the vehicle for the transmission of some rights, bonds of solidarity also tie *matri*kin together. As is found so frequently elsewhere among peoples with a patrilineal organization (e. g. Radcliffe-Brown 1952), the relation between a mother's brother and a sister's child is also, among the Basseri, an indulgent one; and the term "mother's brother", *Dai,* implies easy familiarity. As a term of address it is used frequently to any related elder man, and it is also used "incorrectly" reciprocally by a mother's brother as a term of address to his sister's children (and even occasionally to other children, including his own) on the pattern of the reciprocal grandparent/grandchild usage. The leader of the camp where I spent most of my time is known as *Dai Ghulam,* "uncle Ghulam", by all junior members of the camp; and though this is exceptional, it indicates the importance attached to matrilateral kinship.

Finally, *affinal* relations are also regarded as relations of solidarity and kinship; and they appear to be most effective in establishing political bonds between tents. This effectiveness can only be understood through an investigation of the marriage contract and the transfers involved in marriage, and the authority distribution between the persons concerned.

The authority to make marriage contracts for the members of a household is held by the head of that household. Thus a married man may arrange subsequent marriages for himself, while all women and unmarried boys are subject to the authority of a marriage guardian, who is the head of their household, i. e. the father if he is alive; otherwise a brother or a father's brother. A marriage is thus a transaction between kin groups constituting whole households, and not merely between the contracting spouses. Characteristically, a man refers to his daughter-in-law as *arosam* — "my bride". The rule of exogamy bans only descendants, and ascendants and their collaterals of the first degree. Thus no larger kin group than the "tent", i. e. the elementary family, is normally made relevant to the marriage transaction. Divorce, though legally simple for the man, is a rare occurrence; in one of the two cases I know the marriage was dissolved by the wife.

The marriage contract *(aghd-e-nume)* is often drawn up and written by a non-tribal ritual specialist, a mullah or a holy man. It stipulates certain bride payments, classified by the Basseri as: *shirbahah,* "milk-price", in payment for the girl and the domestic equipment she is expected to bring, and *mahr,* a divorce or widows' insurance or fine, a stipulated sum which is the woman's share of her husband's estate and which is also payable in the event of divorce.

A token gift of a couple of cones of sugar is also given by the groom to the senior mother's brother of the girl.

In the betrothal period the prospective groom is also expected to provide his girl with gifts at all calendrical festivals, and to perform various bride services in the form of continual minor favours to his parents-in-law.

At the time of the wedding, however, all these transactions are completed. There are no outstanding debts either way between affines, apart from the expectation that the father of the girl will return to his son-in-law some of the animals given in bride payment. The woman retains no transferable rights in her natal household. Yet the affinal relation is regarded as warm and enduring by the Basseri, and much emphasis is placed on its maintenance. The levirate and sororate are practised almost without exception, even against the will of the women concerned. Sister exchange marriages *(gav-ba-gav,* "cow-for-cow")* are frequently arranged. And the renewal of affinal ties in each succeeding generation by further marriages is also sought. These subsequent marriages are not regarded as delayed exchange marriages, since the direction of transfer of the woman is immaterial, and not systematically reversed. Their implications are rather like those of marriages between parallel cousins, to counteract the weakening of kin ties that results from increased collateral distance. This tendency to renew affinal ties in every generation may be seen in the genealogical tables given elsewhere (Figs. 2, 10).

The relationship between affines among the Basseri is thus a strong and important one, which people try to maintain through the generations and which is used to reinforce even close matrilateral bonds, and the bonds between close agnatic collaterals. That this should be so may seem surprising. From general anthropological experience one would expect the relation between affines, particularly brothers-in-law, to be one of tension (see e. g. the general formulation by Homans 1950: 250). However, the situation becomes understandable against the background of other features of Basseri organization.

The autonomy, both economic and political, of individual Basseri tents has already been repeatedly emphasized; it is a fundamental feature of Basseri organization. These separate households are structurally united only where there is a community of vested interests between persons in two or more such units. With the pattern of anticipatory inheritance described above, the division of the sibling group between discrete autonomous households is initiated even before the death of the father, and on his death, the division of his property is completed; no estate remains to tie siblings together. Naturally, bonds of sentiment generally remain, but these depend on past experiences and the continuation of good feelings, and do not arise from shared interests in a contemporary situation. Matrilateral kinship similarly does not imply a shared estate of any kind, since the woman retains no transferable rights in her natal home.

The affinal relation, however, does in a sense imply shared rights in an estate — in the woman herself. A woman's father or brother have certain residual rights over her, e. g. as marriage guardians in the event of her widowhood; and the strength of her relations to her kin is maintained by frequent — where possible, daily — visits in her natal tent. At the same time, the honour of her kinsmen is affected by her life and activities; she can both enhance and harm their prestige. Her kinsmen thus retain interest in a married woman, and are to some extent able to exercise control over her; they also desire good relations with her husband to increase this control of theirs over her and her situation.

The husband's rights over his wife of course predominate; but he is completely dependent on her willing co-operation in the daily routine of pastoral nomadism. The considerable autonomy and authority of women in matters within the domestic sphere and family economics clearly arise from this pattern of co-operation and mutual dependence between spouses; it also affects the husband's relations to his affines. Since they hold some rights and have considerable influence over his wife, he is interested in maintaining as close and friendly relations with them as possible; only in concert with them can he hope to control and contain the independence which the wife's economic role gives to her. The close alliance between

34

affines among the Basseri thus springs from the fact that except for lineal ascendants/descendants, they are uniquely united by common interests in an "estate", in this case the person of a woman.

Needless to say, this bond is even stronger in the period between the time when the father-in-law's promise has been given, and the bride is actually transferred. This period usually extends over several years, sometimes even considerably longer; and there is a consistent tendency for the girl's father to be hesitant about terminating it.

For a camp to persist as a social group, its component tents must be knit together by these bonds —agnatic, matrilateral, and particularly affinal. Where such bonds are lacking, there are no other structural ties to hold tent groups larger than the herding units together, and the divisive effect of the daily decision-making with regard to migration and camping will inevitably lead to fission into multiple migrating units.

The heads of households are interested for their own part in main-taining the bonds that counteract the divisive tendencies. In an established tent camp, a man's weight in determining policy, and thus in making the daily decisions that control his and his family's life, is dependent on the extent of his influence over other members of his camp. Therefore men prefer to remain with agnatic and matri-lateral kin, and seek to establish as many strategically placed affinal bonds within the camp as possible. The same is even more important for the camp leader, who desires both to exert maximal influence within the camp, and to hold it together as a group.

The result is a high frequency of endogamy within the camp, implying a high degree of general close-kin marriage and close-knit kinship unity. The census of two camps gives the following frequencies of relation between living spouses:

agnatic cousin	4	29 %	66 %
other cousin	13		
within camp, others	22		
outside camp, within tribe	15	34 %	
outside tribe	5		
Total	59		

35

Attention to the specific constellations of kinsmen in a camp (cf. Fig. 2) show even more clearly than statistical frequencies the importance of affinal ties in cementing the camp, and also the importance of affinal ties in supporting the camp leader in his position. Perhaps the most interesting test of this is the position of the leader in the Darbar camp group where I did most of my work, who in the disposal of his marriageable daughters has disregarded the structural alignments within his camp, and who is experiencing increasing difficulties in controlling the camp members. This camp is too large and too complex in its net of bilateral kinship to be reduced to a single diagram; however, most of the relevant interconnections are shown in the charts describing the herding units of that camp, Fig. 10. The leader of this camp, No. 1, is one of the chief's most trusted men; he has a much wider orientation than most tribesmen and maintains numerous contacts outside the camp and even outside the tribe — many of them in villages. The marriages of his daughters reflect these, his wider interests, as does the fact that he has sent his 14-year-old only son to school in a town; but his position within the camp has been severely weakened by these dispositions. Without a resident son, he relies on the sons of his herding unit partner No. 2 as shepherds (while employing a servant mainly for domestic tasks). This places him in a position of immediate dependence on No. 2, which continually embarrasses him in his role as camp leader. More importantly his wider ties within the camp are critically weakened, and in the period of my field work he experienced one defection from the camp, by No. 5, and several tests of strength with No. 10, twice leading to the latter's temporary separation from the rest of the camp.

Of his six daughters, three have been married but one is deceased. The first marriage was very properly to the eldest son of No. 8, who is a senior man with six sons and four daughters and is No. 1's MoBrSo and SiHu. The camp leader's second daughter is married in the town of Marvdasht. On the death of the first daughter, he denied his son-in-law the customary right to her marriageable sister, and gave that girl, his third daughter, instead to the schoolteacher in the chief's brother's village. The three younger daughters are not yet marriageable. So far, No. 1's strategic position in the senior generation has not been maintained in the junior generation, and by the affinal ties now being established the centres of influence are shifting. His

The Darbar camp on migration, near Jahrom.

Tents of a herding unit, near Jahrom.

11-12- year- old daughter has been promised to the son of No. 3, who is No. 1's MoSiSo and SiHu. This man, who is also a trusted servant of the chief, is No. 1's main and crucial supporter in camp. No. 7, through his devotion to the chief as the latter's hunting companion and story-teller, is also committed to No. 1 as the recognized headman, but exerts little influence in camp. The main foci of opposition are No. 5 and No. 10, independent of each other. No. 9's brother is betrothed to No. 5's daughter; through his hesitance to formalize this promise No. 5 sought to exert influence over No. 9, and on to No. 7's sons, who for various personal reasons are in opposition to their father. All these persons are of Qashqai extraction, like No. 5 himself. However, by threats of brute force No. 9 was able to extract a formal betrothal promise, and when No. 5 defected from the tribe to spend the summer in the Arab *sarhad* near Fassa, he failed in spite of all efforts to carry others from the camp with him, and had to separate his flock from the larger herd of his herding unit and leave by himself.

The other main focus of expressed opposition, No. 10, is similarly unconnected with the camp leader No. 1 by close ties either of kinship or marriage. No. 10's strength in part depends on his having retained his married sons and son-in-law in his own, exclusive herding unit. His main attachment to the rest of the camp is a double link to No. 2 — through his wife's sister, who was an unwilling leviratic bride of No. 2, and as father-in-law to one of No. 2's sons. Throughout the spring of 1958 No. 10 exerted a magnetic influence by holding back on promising his marriageable daughter and son's daughter to anyone. The main suitors were the camp leader's widowed son-in-law, on his own behalf, and No. 2's step-son, who offered a sister exchange marriage with his son and daughter. Once in the middle of migration, No. 10 put his influence to a test by refusing to break camp when the camp leader had decided to migrate. Fortunately for the latter, No. 3 arrived with orders from the chief that the camp *should* move on; this limited the defection to No. 10's own herding unit, who overtook the rest of the camp two days later.

A month later, close to the summer pastures, No. 10 decided to follow a different route from that which the rest of the camp were to take. Instructions from the chief again supported the camp leader in his decision, and kept the other herding units within the fold.

Before the separation, the two suitors pressed to have No. 10's promises confirmed in a betrothal ceremony. In this they were strongly supported by the camp leader, perhaps because such an irrevocable promise would at lest to some extent reduce No. 10's arbitrary influence. This was successful, and the group remained camped an extra day at the place of separation to celebrate the betrothal. Later, No. 2 and his sons, and several other herding units, joined No. 10 in relatively low-lying summer pastures, and only 11 tents in all accompanied the camp leader to the usual high mountain pastures of the group. Though dispersal is common in the couple of summer months and does not indicate dissolution of the camp, the weakness of the camp leader's position was further revealed by this. In contrast, camp leaders with a more strategic kinship position, maintained by optimal renewal and distribution of affinal ties, appear to exert a stronger influence over the members of their camp group.

One may from the preceding discussion discern three kinds of bonds which have the effect of tying households together in a tent camp: those of patrilineal, matrilineal, and affinal kinship. In addition, occasional service contracts may incorporate shepherds and servants, and their dependents, into camps where they have no ties of kinship, though distant kin are preferred for such purposes. Finally, a camp's composition may be affected by structurally unpredictable factors such as personal friendships, or the request by refugees from other tribes for political asylum. This last variable factor has, incidentally, been of unusual importance for the Darbar camp group where I spent most of my time, since it was the normal camp of residence for the chief, and most refugees seek the presence of the chief and thus tend more frequently to be incorporated into his camp. For certain aspects of recruitment and internal structure, this camp is thus a-typical and will be treated apart from my other material.

It should be noted that the kinds of claims, the rights and duties expected between kinsmen within a camp, are the same whether the relative is a patrilateral or matrilateral collateral, or an affine. This was illustrated in the freedom of association in herding units (p. 22), it is apparent from the patterns of spontaneous and routinized co-operation during migration and in camp, and in the association and relations of comradeship and respect between kinsmen in general.

38

That this should be so is consistent with other features of the system. Because of the pattern of anticipatory inheritance all relations between persons of different tents are essentially divested of relevance to any material estate (the sharing of pasture rights is described below, pp. 55ff. and never serves to differentiate camp group members); therefore relationships within a camp are not greatly affected by the patrilineal inheritance rules. There is thus no apparent difference in the kind and degree of expected identification and loyalty due to kinsmen, no distinctions in the services or respect due to senior relatives, whether they are patrikin, matrikin, or affines. As within the tent, where the husband and wife are nearly equal in the domestic sphere, though the husband is absolute head of the household in all external relations, so also in the camp: a bilateral system of duties and relations is observed inside the camp, while its outer boundaries are clearly conceived in patrilineal terms.

The composition of some camps is given in Fig. 2, which shows the relationship between the heads of households in each of five different, moderately small camps. The corresponding net of relationships in the Darbar camp can be constructed from Fig. 10.

The bonds of patrilineal, matrilineal, and affinal kinship are all exemplified in each of the camps. The Basseri themselves frequently speak of a camp, especially for purposes of placing it in relation to other camps of the tribe, as if all members of the camp belong to a single patrilineage, which again forms a segment of larger lineages in a merging series, culminating in the patrilineal point of origin of all Basseri. Such patrilineages are clearly visible as cores in the camp groups A-E; though reduced to a minority in camps A and C they are still recognizable and contain, by definition, the leader of the camp. However, the same persons who express the view that camp groups are exclusive patrilineages will also emphasize the bilateral, "family" nature of their camp; and they never differentiate certain rights and duties as obtaining specifically and exclusively between patrikin.

The place of the patrilineal principle in the organization of the camp can be made clear only in relation to other factors that structure the group, mainly, the high endogamous frequency. In camp D, the genealogical positions of the *wives* of all the heads of households are shown, as well as the position of a few collateral agnates who are

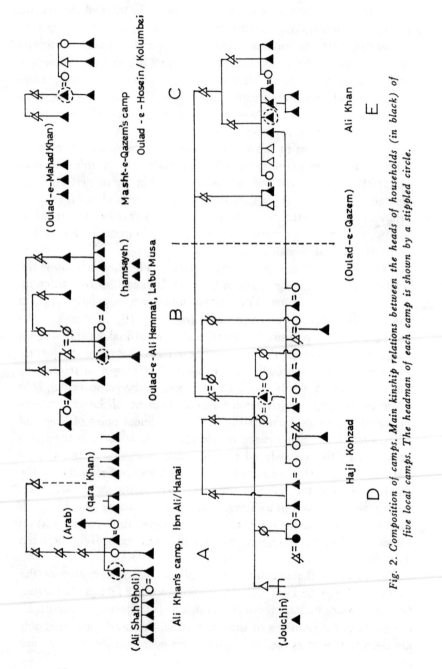

Fig. 2. Composition of camps. Main kinship relations between the heads of households (in black) of five local camps. The headman of each camp is shown by a stippled circle.

not members of the camp. The picture this camp presents agrees with incomplete information from other camps and has not been selected for its particular fit — complete census material is difficult to obtain for political and taxation reasons, and happened to be available from this camp due to good relations with informants. The same features are also visible in the Darbar camp, Fig. 10.

The endogamous character of the camp group D is clearly visible — it nearly approaches an in-breeding, self-perpetuating population. The strong impression of a patrilineal core which the other charts give, and which the Basseri occasionally emphasize, is deceptive, since agnatic ties in no sense predominate over other ties of kinship. Chart D could with equal success be re-drawn to give an impression of a group built around matri-lineages. The correct and complete picture of the kinship composition of camps is one that reveals their character as bilateral, nearly self-perpetuating kin groups.

In such a group, the strongly bilateral authority distribution that characterizes the domestic domain and relations between close relatives can be extended to the political sphere within the camp without coming into conflict with an explicit patrilineal ideology, or with the principle of patriliny as applied in the higher echelons of the tribal organization. Matrilateral and affinal kinsmen in camp are for the most part also patri-kinsmen, and identification and solidarity that derives from the former relationship may, when necessary, also be justified by the latter.

The bilateral structure of camps also explains why the continual formation of patrilineal nuclei of fathers and sons (cf. p. 30) does not result in the development of lineages. Such a development requires that the social distance between collateral agnatic lines should be maintained, and increase with each generation, i.e. be proportionate to genealogical distance, or, put differently, it depends on a process of continual segmentation. But this does not take place where close kin marriage continually re-combines the collateral lines and no systematic differentiation is made between rights and duties implied by patrilateral and matrilateral relations. The segmentation implicit in the patrilineal framework is thus blurred by the importance of ties to matrikin and affines, and the camp emerges as a basically unsegmented group. This does not mean that the camp is not at any one time divided into various kinds of sub-groups. But such sub-groups

41

are impermanent, and either without clear boundaries, such as the spheres of influence of prominent men, or they are clearly associated with a specific and limited activity, such as herding. They thus do not constitute segments in any more general sociological sense.

The physical aspect of a pitched camp largely confirms this lack of segmentation. Quite clearly, physical distance is used to express social distance. Thus in one case a fight broke out between two households just after the daily migration, when the donkeys had been unloaded and driven off but before the tents had been pitched. As soon as the fighting had been stopped by the intervention of others, each family dragged their belongings away in opposite directions as far as was feasible, and the next day they pitched their tents in opposite ends of the camp. Improvement in relations was indicated by their moving closer together again.

But though distance is a clear social idiom, the relative location of the tents of a camp is not such as to give any clear expression of its internal structure; and the regularities that do occur can be explained by purely practical considerations. Thus, the members of a herding unit must camp together, since they wish to be close to their animals, mixed in a common herd, at milking time and through-out the nights. Within this group, where there are three or more tents, their relative positions are generally constant — but this reflects the ties of kinship and economic dependence within the herding unit, and not in the camp as a whole. On the other hand, it is convenient to keep the tents of different herding units at a minimal distance of 20-30 meters from each other, to avoid the mixing of herds. But the relative positions of such herding units in the larger scheme of the whole camp is relatively variable. Many camp sites restrict by their shape the possible pattern of distribution of tents. And even on open, level steppe, where the tents of herding units tend to form small semicircles within a larger semicircle formed by the whole camp, the relative positions of herding units vary from one day to the next. Where consistent patterns of relative closeness or distance were observed, special practical reasons were found, such as joint camel herding, or avoidance to prevent fights between mature stallions, etc. Spacial distribution does not appear to reflect any permanent lines of cleavage within the camp.

The same unsegmented character of the camp group is revealed

42

during migration. The herds travel slowly along the hillside or on the open steppe, grazing, while the donkey and camel caravan carrying the nomads' goods proceeds more quickly and follows the main roads and paths. Though all the tents of a camp are struck more or less simultaneously a little before sunrise, the packing and loading takes about an hour and some families finish before others. These move off as soon as they are ready — in fact it apears to be impossible to hold back the loaded beasts — so the departure times of the first and the last household in a large camp may differ by as much as half an hour. The caravan itself is thus spread out over at least a mile; within this the pack animals of each tent are kept close together and those of members of the same herding unit tend to travel as a group. The mounted men generally leave their family in charge of the property as soon as the group is under way, and proceed up to the head of the caravan. When the time comes to choose a camp site, the riders in the lead make the decision, and disperse over the chosen area to stake out their claims to the better localities for their own tents and the tents of their herding units. In the Darbar camp, at least, there was a relatively consistent pattern whereby the leader was the last to depart from the camp site, lending a hand to other late departers who might be in difficulty. He then slowly made his way up through the whole caravan, reaching its head (together with his wife, who was the only woman who rode a mule) well before it was time to choose a camp site. I do not know whether this is also the pattern in other groups.

The daily and unavoidable decisions on which the persistence of the group itself depends concern whether to break camp and to migrate, by which route to migrate, and where to pitch the new camp. Particularly the first of these is a recurring decision that every day re-tests the cohesion of the group. As I have shown above, the camp leader lacks means whereby he can dictate a decision to the group or to any of its constituent tents; he must therefore every day succeed in obtaining unanimity among its members. The process whereby this is achieved is one of the fundamental social processes in nomad society and has, as I shall attempt to show, very fundamental implications also for their wider political system. It is therefore important to describe in some detail the decision-making process.

Various features of the process strike a Western participant observer

43

strongly, mainly the avoidance of any kind of assembly containing all or a majority of the heads of households concerned, and the frustrating suspension of decisions whereby matters are discussed endlessly without clear statements of position, and often without a clear conclusion, so that even experienced members of the group retire in the evening without knowing whether the tents will be struck next morning.

The lack of assemblies relates to the nature of "influence". The kind of influence exercised by the camp leader and by other prominent men derives only to a slight extent from absolute characteristics or qualifications of the man, and predominantly from his personal connections, mainly of kinship, as a set of dyadic relations to a medley of camp members. The Basseri themselves sometimes simplify the picture somewhat and say: "A man's influence depends not on what he has here (pointing to the head) but on what he has here (pointing to the genitalia)!" Married sons and daughters spread his influence through the camp, and these and other kinsmen and affines form the web through which he may seek to dominate.

It is therefore important for a leader to avoid any large assembly of camp members, where each voice would be more nearly equal. Instead he seeks persons out singly or in small gatherings where his friends and kinsmen are in majority; within such a group his influence may prevail. These men can then go out to similar groups of their kith and kin, where they can speak with greater force, strengthened by the knowledge of speaking the mind of another majority, and thus disseminate the originator's suggestions further.

The avoidance of a clear statement of decision is thereby made more understandable. Though most speakers seek to reveal the trend of their preference, they always retain counter-arguments in their statements. The opinions of other persons seem to be evaluated by their differential response to the first speaker's various arguments implying the different alternatives, and not necessarily by the conclusion implied by the balance of opinions expressed by them. In such fashion no person ends up having clearly committed himself to what may turn out to be a minority opinion; his own statements have consistently contained arguments both for and against, and their relative weight has never been fully revealed. Lack of agreement is revealed by continued conversation around the subject, never by flat

44

contradiction. And the "arguments" presented in such conversations need not be factors of real relevance to the decision, but are often just convenient ways in which one or another decision may be implied. Not only does the frustrated anthropologist remain in the dark whether he will have to pack his stuff and move on next morning; he cannot even learn about herding and nomadic life from these hour-long discussions, when points which are bandied about and emphasized by all turn out to be without substantive relevance to the problem. A gross example is the frequent argument heard in such discussions that there is no water available ahead, and so it is difficult to move on next morning. My naive questions the first time I heard this, of how this might improve during the next few days, or else how we would ever be able to proceed, were dismissed by all as irrelevant, and irritated rather than embarrassed the speakers. Another time the whole camp reached unanimity around the statement that we could not in any circumstance move the next day, since it was the day of Ali's death (though many speakers got this confused with the martyrdom of Husain). But next morning it looked like rain, and tents were struck and the camp moved on with no further mention of Ali.

Conversations on the topic of camping or migrating next day usually start in the early afternoon, and unless a clear lack of agreement is revealed, the topic remains secondary, though frequently touched upon by oblique remarks, throughout the evening. Where no agreement is apparent, the intensity of interaction between tents starts mounting around sunset; there is much social visiting where the conversation quickly is made relevant explicitly or implicitly to the topic on everybody's mind. Usually a clear trend of opinion does emerge, but sometimes one or a few of the influential persons remain adamant in spite of pressure, and the camp members retire late without having reached a decision. On such mornings, there is much consultation between the different shepherds, and between them and the heads of households, since the direction in which they depart, before daybreak, depends upon, and is indicative though not conclusive of, whether they expect the camp to move or stay. If all the herds go off in the general direction of the migration route, there is usually an uneasy period of mutual peeping through the tent cloth without making any further move; finally one or two courageous proponents of migration will strike their tents, and within a couple of minutes the other tents will almost always follow suit. If on the other hand the herds disperse in all directions, some of them demonstratively back-tracking, the leader, if he has been in favour of migrating, will quickly place himself among the majority by coming out of his tent and showing himself idle.

The route, where a choice exists, and occasionally the projected camp site, are often chosen incidentally to the evening's decision on migrating or camping. Where this is not the case, decision-making follows a similar pattern. Occasionally, one or several men at the head of the caravan would spread out over a possible camp site without succeeding in drawing the caravan with them off the main road. In such cases they sometimes camped there with their herding unit, the rest of the group proceeding to the first possible subsequent site and camping there. More frequently, the hopeful but unsuccessful leaders would discover their mistake soon enough so they could overtake the others and inform them that the camp site was no good this year.

The picture of the camp as the primary community of Basseri society may be rounded off by a general characterization of its relations with the outside. A fundamental feature is the relative isolation of each camp. Its members have intimate and frequent interaction with each other, and their multiplex interrelations are frequently activated, e.g. in the decision-making process described above. Relations with outsiders, on the other hand, are very few and interaction very infrequent. The camp members react continually, in a complex manner, to the physical environment; they co-operate in sub-groups and as a whole unit; and the migrations themselves may in a sense be regarded as large-scale, nearly daily occasions when the unity and the distinctiveness of the group is asserted by its constancy in changing localities, its difference from the sedentary communities by or through which the caravan frequently passes, etc. But social contacts outside, even with other Basseri groups, are largely avoided, to such an extent that intercommunication between camps is poor even when they are located close to each other for longer periods. After two weeks' residence with the Darbar camp on the Mansurabad plain I visited another group that had been camped an equal length of time within clear sight about three miles away on the plain. It turned out that they had no knowledge of my presence — though the fact of my residence "as a Basseri" with a nomad family was invariably a topic of great interest to all who heard of it. The nomads' ignorance of persons in the many Basseri camps we saw and camped close by on our way, and even of the identity of other camps, was a constant reminder of the social isolation in which each camp lives.

This isolation is partly a product of the barriers of suspicion and fear with which the camp members surround themselves. While relations within the group are characterized by the diffuse and embracing mutual trust appropriate between close kin, all outsiders that are not closely related are regarded with the utmost reserve. The camp is very unwilling to admit new members, even as hired shepherds; they fear the possible "troubles" that a stranger in their midst may cause. Other camps are suspected of theft and banditry; with some justification every herd-owner feels that outside his camp he is surrounded by a hostile world full of sheep-thieves and robbers. At night even adult men are afraid to go far outside the circle of tents, and no one ever pitches his tent alone at any distance from the others, for fear of nightly isolation and consequent vulnerability to thieves. Clearly, though thefts of animals do occur, the excessive fear of thieves is reminiscent of witchcraft beliefs in many respects. Persons who do not fear the isolation make themselves liable to accusations of theft, and the general emphasis on the camp as a small nucleus of human warmth surrounded by evil corresponds closely to its structural position.

Apart from this generalized and mainly symbolic identification of members with the camp community, the group is rarely mobilized as a corporate unit in conflict situations with other groups. The prevailing fear and suspicion keeps groups at a reasonable distance from each other, and violent conflicts occur only rarely. Fights with sticks and stones may occasionally develop over pastures between shepherds from different camps, and when these take place sufficiently close to camp the whole group may join in the fray. I never observed such a case in the field; the Darbar camp had been involved in one the previous year. The general topic of conflicts between camps, and other groups, and their solution, is discussed in connection with the description of the political organization.

Chapter IV

TRIBE AND SECTIONS

The description so far has proceeded from elementary to compound units in the Basseri social system; I have tried to build from the basic units of *tents,* with their internal organization, through *herding units* to *camps* as the primary communities of nomad society. These groups have all been described in terms of the processes by which they emerge and maintain themselves; and I believe that the picture which has emerged up to the camp level is essentially common to all the pastoral nomads of the South Persian area. The differences that do exist between nomads of that area have to do mainly with the tribal organization *above* that level, though these differences do also have repercussions on the form of groups on the lower levels.

In presenting my material on the higher levels of organization among the Basseri, it is convenient to shift the point of view and describe the system from the outside, or above, regarding all smaller units as parts of a delimited whole: the Basseri tribe. The following description is thus specific for this one case; I shall attempt later to show that the Basseri organization may be regarded as an example of a *type* of organization which characterizes some, but not all, of the nomads of the South Persian area.

This change in viewpoint produces a break in the analysis between the processes described so far, in the smaller groups, and the processes which operate on the higher levels. However, I argue that this break is not merely an artifact of the mode of description, but represents the articulation point between processes of fundamentally different kinds; and that basic features of Basseri organization are better understood when this break is emphasized, rather than slurred over by a simple ordering of groups in a typologic series of inclusiveness. While groups up to the level of camps depend on processes that have their source within tents and elementary families, other processes emanate from the central chief of the Basseri, and have their source in part outside the Basseri tribe. I shall try to show that these two different kinds of processes articulate first and foremost on the level between camps and sections.

We are here first concerned with the analysis of the formal hierarchy of groups and sub-groups by which the tribesmen are ordered into a tribe and through which their chief exercises his administrative powers. This is in essence a simple schema. The Basseri tribe of Fars regard themselves as an *Il* (tribe) divided into 12 proper *Tira* (descent groups). An intermediate level of segment often referred to as *Taife* which is found among the Arab tribes of the area does not exist among the Basseri, who regard the term *Taife* as an uncommon synonym for *Tira*.

The different *Tira* of the Basseri, which I refer to in this book as *sections*, are structurally equivalent but of highly variable size. Most of them are thus subdivided into groups called *Oulad* (family). Some sections contain no such internal subdivisions, others contain as many as six oulads. As well as differing in size and number of subdivisions, the sections also differ somewhat in prestige — partly because of differences in wealth, partly because of differing genealogical traditions, especially the fact that the chiefly dynasty sprang from a branch of one of them, the Kolumbei.

Below the oulad the chief takes no formal cognizance of any grouping above the household, so the formal framework of groups and sub-groups is, in descending order, tribe - section - oulad - tent.

The following list of sections, oulads and tents is copied from a census made by order of the Basseri chief in 1951 by the chief's scribe. All the groups designated are still in existence; but their sizes have changed slightly, some by growth and others by suffering a decline. Included in the list is also the section Il-e-Khas, which joined the tribe after 1951, and is represented here by its 1958 population figure, based on my own census.

However, these groups are not only abstract administrative devices; they are also living and self-perpetuating units. Each of the sections, and their component oulads, have their traditional histories, some of

50

Section	Oulad	No. of tents
Kolumbei	Oulad-e-Yusuf	80
	Oulad-e-Qazem	50
	Oulad-e-Hosein	52
	Oulad-e-Mahmud	13
	Oulad-e-Mahad Khan	43
Abduli	Ali Marduni	89
	Moradi	59
	Shahbani	{ 46
		59 }
	Abdul Qazemi	42
	Bala Velayati	51
	Oulad-e-Khan Mahad	70
Labu Musa	Jaffar-e-Ghambari	126
	Rostam-e-Shiravani	101
	Ahmad-e-Shiravani	74
Jouchin	Korejei	91
	Gulestani	65
	Oulad-e-Reza	42
	Oulad-e-Qorban	43
	Oulad-e-Mokhtar	81
	Oulad-e-Qazem	62
Ali Shah Gholi		77
Zohrabi		53
Farhadi	Bahmani	65
	Farhadi	42
Ahl-e-Gholi		39
Hanai		60
Ali Ghambari		75
Karemi		200
Salvestuni		26
Il-e-Khas	Eskandar	{ 100*
	Qader Ali	}
Darbar-e-Zarghami		45
Khavanin		31

* 1958 population figures.

them of importance to the tribe as a whole, some known and of interest only to the members. In place of the strict structural equivalence they are given in the formal system, these traditions differentiate them and interconnect them in numerous ways.

In various versions, the tradition survives that the sections of the Basseri hail mainly from two different origins, one native to the area and one intrusive. The former are grouped together as Ali Mirzai; the latter claim descent from Weis, who is supposed to have come from Khorasan. The Ali Mirzai came under the Weisi only three generations ago — but both groups claim always to have been known as Basseri. Certain other sections have different origins; thus the Ahl-e-Gholi are supposed to be derived from the Qarachei Qashqai, the Salvestuni from the village of Sarvestan, and the Ali Shah Gholi and possibly the Hanai from the Arabs. Groups carrying the same names and identified as collateral are also found in different tribes: the Ali Shah Gholi form a section of the Abdul Yusufi *Taife* of the Arabs, while another section of the Arabs is called Hanai. The Hanai also occur as a section in the Isfahan area. The Jouchin oulad Korejei is found also among the Arabs and among the Qashqai, while they and many other sections have branches in the Isfahan-Yazd-i-Khast area. The whole Il-e-Khas migrated from the Basseri lands to that area in A. H. 1282 and were brought back only a few years ago; the Bala Velayati oulad of the Abduli (all land north of the Qashqai is known among the Basseri as Bala Velayat — "Upper homeland" or "Upper region") returned from that same area some 60 years ago, while groups of Hanai, Il-e-Khas, and various Ali Mirzai sections including the Husein Ahmedi no longer in existence among the Basseri proper, are still found there.

The genetic relations of the present sections of the tribe may thus be summarized as in Fig. 3, dotted arrows indicating derivation by broad processes of recruitment, solid lines proper genealogical segmentation.

These genetic relations do not, however, affect the formal structural equivalence of sections in the chief's administrative hierarchy.

The differing traditions of oulads are of little importance to outsiders, since their identification with their section clearly overrides the other identifications that might be implied by such traditions. None the less, there is a tendency towards a blurring of the formal scheme

52

Sayyids writing the marriage contract during a betrothal ceremony.

*Filling skin bags with drinking water.
The camp is often pitched several
miles from the source of water.*

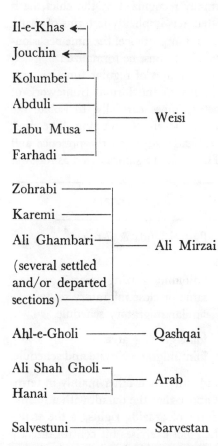

Fig. 3. Genetic relations of Basseri sections.

on the oulad level, but mainly because of the variable meanings of the term *oulad* itself. While the word *tira*, the section, refers strictly to the one level of segmentation represented by the twelve groups listed above, an oulad may be a group on any level of subdivision below the section, in terms of strict descent or in more general terms of residence and political unity. Persons will thus on occasion refer to a great variety of "oulads" that are not on the preceding list, and that sometimes turn out to be the dispersed patrilineal descendants of a certain ancestor, sometimes a genealogically compound camp group.

Finally, though the groupings between the level of the oulad and the individual tent are not formally recognized by the chief, he is largely familiar with them, and often acts implicitly in terms of them. With changing relations of growth and importance, the time occasionally comes when such implicit recognition must be formalized.

But before these processes of growth, and of regular function, can be described, it is necessary to return to the formal framework of organization and analyse its structure more carefully, to isolate the defining characteristics of the various levels of grouping. The most important of these have to do with leadership, and the presence and nature of a joint physical estate. These may be summarized as follows:

group	leadership	estate
tribe (*Il*)	chief	Basseri lands & *il-rah*
section (*tira*)	—	adjoining grazing areas same or close migratory route similar migratory schedule
oulad	headman	joint grazing area joint migratory route and schedule.

Though the Basseri themselves identify each other mainly in terms of the sections, it is clear from the above that the oulad, with a formal leader and a joint estate in the form of grazing rights, is the structurally more important group. The chief exercises his control directly through the oulads, and the grouping of such oulads into leaderless sections, whose estates are the sum of the estates of the component oulads, has little importance in the formal system.

The grazing rights held by the oulads are a vitally important estate which obviously provides the basis for the pastoral adaptation. The way the S. Persian system of nomadism has developed, no pastures are "owner-less"; so without access through his oulad to such an estate, the nomad would be unable to subsist. But it is important to realize that these rights vested in an oulad are *allocated* rights to *usufruct,* not absolute property rights. Though the nomads themselves usually speak of pasture rights as if they were immutable through time and based on age-old usage, they are in fact subject to arbitrary reallot-

54

ment by the chief. Thus ten years before my field work, when rapid growth following the resumption of full nomadism in 1941 had led to shortage of traditional pastures for some oulads and surplus for others, the chief called all the headmen together and instituted a sweeping reform. In this reform the whole pattern of distribution of pastures and routes was revised, and while many groups were allocated their traditional pastures, others were given entirely new localities. Similarly, when the Il-e-Khas returned from the Isfahan area a few years ago, adjustments were made in the pastures of other groups so that a migratory schedule was cleared for the newcomers, and a solid block of pastures provided for them in the summer area.

As well as having an estate, the oulad also has a formally recognized leader in its *katkhoda* or headman. Within their own camp such headmen have a position roughly like that of other camp leaders; but their position *vis-à-vis* the chief is clearly marked off, and by him they are held responsible equally for all members of their oulad, regardless of its division into different camps.

Thus each oulad is a division of one of the named sections of the tribe, and thus has its defined place in the formal tribal system. It constitutes a group with defined usufruct rights to pastures and a designated headman, and is thus a product of the chief's administration. He formally defines its membership, leadership, and estate. But in doing this he merely recognizes and utilizes certain rules and groupings that are a part of the Basseri social system. They are not his creations, though he gives them a formal regularity and perhaps a field of relevance that they would otherwise lack.

The principle which the chief draws out and makes the basis for his recognition of groups and allocation of rights is the patrilineal principle. We have seen that such a patrilineal principle has little relevance in creating political bonds of solidarity between agnates. It is, however, the recognized principle of succession; and so membership in an administrative group, and the transmission of usufruct rights to pastures, naturally follows this principle.

A man's rights in an oulad thus depend on his patrilineal descent, on his ability to "prove" his rights by means of a pedigree that others will recognize, describing his descent from an apical ancestor of the oulad. While many informants could give these pedigrees with considerable ease, often leading back 8 or 10 generations, they proved

55

unable to expand them into true ramifying genealogies of the whole oulad. On the background of my previous experience with Pathans, who might have difficulties giving good pedigrees but readily outlined the whole segmentary charter of their descent group (Barth 1959: 22 ff.), this inability of the Basseri was in the field situation both puzzling and frustrating. When asked to designate the main segments of an oulad, different informants would give widely different pictures, confuse levels of segmentation, and later constantly return to the theme, having remembered further names. The pedigrees I collected also show a surprising lack of fit with the recognized and formalized pattern of grouping into oulads and sections. Thus repeatedly one or more names would be given *above* that of the epinymic ancestor of the oulad — but without leading to any common ancestor of the whole section. Quite often, pedigrees would end inexplicably without having reached the epinymic ancestor; and not infrequently authoritative pedigrees lead to an immigrant ancestor, unconnected by descent or supposed marriage with other oulads of the section (e. g. Korejei oulad of Jouchin, or Ali Marduni oulad of Abduli; cf. Fig. 4).

The most complete and complex genealogical charter was collected for the Kolumbei. Though I was given various versions of it, there was basic agreement on most of its features and the version that is reproduced below (Fig. 5) may be regarded as "correct". The upper part of this charter, defining the relations between Kolumbei oulads and the dynastic line, was also the only one about which there was some interest and agreement outside the section itself, in the tribe in general. In this section, too, the subdivision into defined oulads and the division of pastures between them are the clearest. In some other groups (e. g. Labu Musa, and some Jouchin, cf. below), this division does not seem complete, and the delimited group owning an estate is the section itself, rather than its less clearly delimited primary oulads.

In every case, however, we are dealing at some level with a clearly delimited unit — usually the oulad, sometimes the section — membership in which is transmitted patrilineally, and the members of which have at any time, by allotment of the chief, exclusive pasture rights in specified areas at specified times. These rights are a prerequisite to the pursuit of a pastoral economy; so every Basseri herd-owner must obtain them by being a member of one such oulad.

56

Fig. 4. Pedigrees from some Basseri oulads.

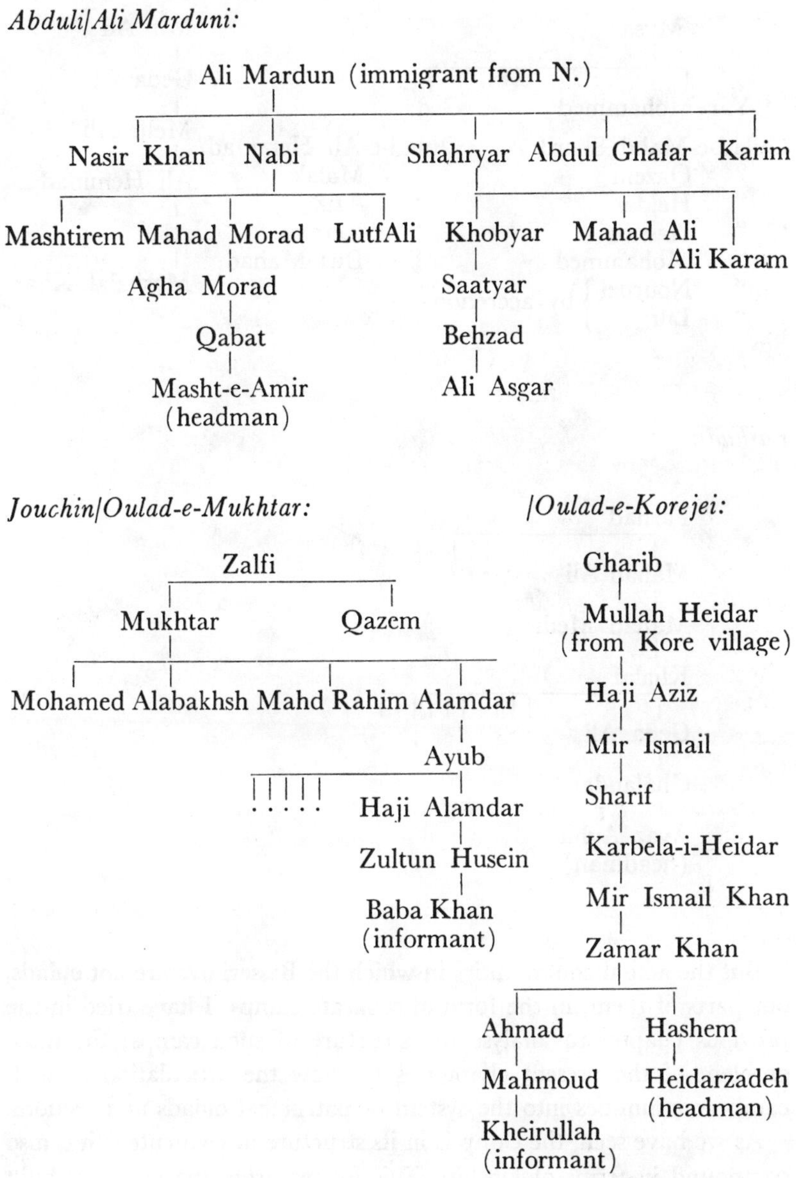

Abduli/Ali Marduni:

```
                    Ali Mardun (immigrant from N.)
          ┌──────────┬──────────┬──────────┬────────┬────────┐
      Nasir Khan    Nabi    Shahryar   Abdul  Ghafar  Karim
      ┌───────┬───────┴─────────┐        │
  Mashtirem Mahad Morad      LutfAli  Khobyar  Mahad Ali
          Agha Morad                  Saatyar        Ali Karam
             Qabat                     Behzad
        Masht-e-Amir                  Ali Asgar
         (headman)
```

Jouchin/Oulad-e-Mukhtar:

```
                    Zalfi
          ┌──────────────────────┐
       Mukhtar               Qazem
   ┌───────┬──────────┬─────────┐
Mohamed Alabakhsh Mahd Rahim Alamdar
                              Ayub
      | | | | |            Haji Alamdar
      · · · · ·
                         Zultun Husein
                          Baba Khan
                          (informant)
```

/Oulad-e-Korejei:

```
              Gharib
          Mullah Heidar
        (from Kore village)
            Haji Aziz
            Mir Ismail
              Sharif
         Karbela-i-Heidar
          Mir Ismail Khan
            Zamar Khan
          ┌──────────┐
        Ahmad      Hashem
       Mahmoud   Heidarzadeh
                  (headman)
      Kheirullah
      (informant)
```

(Continued overleaf)

Labu Musa: *Oulad-e-Ali Hemmad:*

		Mir Ali

Musa
```
        ┌─────────────────────┬──────────────┐
   Yar Mohammed                           Geda
Oulad-e-Mahd Sharif              Oulad-e-Ali Hemmad
   "     Qazem                      "      Malak
   "     Heidar                     "      Aziz
   "     Hassan                     "      Keram
   "     Mohammed                   "      Dus Mahad
   "     Nouruzi ⎫ by accretion
   "     Lur     ⎭
```

Mir Ali
|
Geda Ali
|
Mehr Ali
|
Ali Hemmad
|
Asad
|
Mashalaf Khan

Farhadi:

```
Farhad
 │              │ │ │
Mahad Ali       · · ·
 │
Mahad Medi
 │
Khalaf
 │          │ │ │ │ │ │ │ │ │ │
Geda Ali    · · · · · · · · · ·
 │
Ghalandar
 │
Avaz Agha
(headman)
```

But the actual communities in which the Basseri live are not oulads, but parts of them, in the form of separate camps. I have tried in the previous chapter to analyse the structure of such camps; the main problem of the present chapter is to show the articulation of such camp communities into the system of patrilineal oulads and sections.

As we have seen, the camp is in its structure unsegmented; it is also compound in terms of kinship. This follows from the way it is built up, through the exercise of influence by senior men over bilateral

58

kinsmen and perhaps particularly over affines. Because of these processes by which they are built up, such camps will never constitute patrilineal descent segments of a larger oulad — they are recruited by principles entirely different from the rule of patrilineal succession defining the oulad; yet they are integrated into an administrative framework which in the definition of its larger units is based explicitly on this rule.

One might think that this situation might be conveniently treated by means of the familiar concept of matrilateral grafting, whereby non-agnates are attached to a patrilineal core and have their position in a wider political schema defined by the descent position of this core. However, such a presentation would do violence to the present material by imputing differential rights to membership within a camp, and by disguising the basic difference in the processes involved in camp formation and the formation of oulads. Instead, I shall focus the analysis precisely on this difference, in an attempt thereby to clarify a greater variety of features of Basseri organization.

Let us begin with the position of an ordinary member of the tribe. As his birth-right he obtains rights to the pastures of his oulad. These are his by virtue of his pedigree and secured for him by the chief's authority; he need not exercise these rights through any larger corporate descent group. He is thus free to move quite independently within his oulad; with respect to economic rights, and thus for important political purposes, the oulad is an internally unstructured aggregate of persons. Its boundaries are defined in patrilineal terms, but it also seems that an individual's rights can with little difficulty be transferred to another oulad of his own section — here a segmentary principle holds true, and rights within a segment are agreed by all to imply, in principle, rights within the homologous larger unit. In the illustrations already given, for example, the brother of Haji Kohzad of Oulad-e-Qasem Kolumbei (Fig. 2 camp D) lives with his descendants among the Oulad-e-Mahad Khan Kolumbei; while conversely three tents in the Oulad-e-Hosein (Fig. 2 camp C) are Oulad-e-Mahad Khan by descent.

For an outsider by descent to gain entry in a section and its oulads is, on the other hand, very difficult, and requires the confirmation by the headman of a unanimous acceptance within an oulad. But once such entry has been achieved, it implies no transmitted stigma for the descendants, who become full and equal members of the oulad, without being fictionally assimilated to its genealogy. For this latter reason it is possible to identify those who have entered a group from the outside, and their descendants, at least for some generations. Their numbers seem to be small — thus of the c. 100 tents now under the Ali Marduni (Abduli) headman, only 5 or 6 do not belong by agnatic descent to the group, while of the 48 tents under Avaz Agha Farhadpur, none are not Farhadi.

The movements of a man are thus essentially restricted by the limits of the oulad or section with whom he shares inherited pasture rights; but within this unit he is free to attach himself to any kind of grouping. Thus camps can form by the processes previously described, without any reference to agnatic relationships, so long as their personnel is drawn from within the appropriate maximal unit. This is one reason why the matrilateral and affinal ties that connect members to the camp group can not be analysed in terms of the concept of matrilateral grafting. These men already have rights, they do not obtain them through women; and their association with their affines is based on the factors expounded in chapter III, not on an economic dependence situation. Thus in Fig. 2, all the heads of households in camp B are Labu Musa, so those with only affinal ties to other members of the camp are still their equals in terms of inherited pasture rights. Similarly, all heads of household in camps C, D and E are Kolumbei. The special situation among the Hanai, exemplified by camp A, will be discussed shortly (pp. 68-69).

In other words, though the membership of camps is drawn from an oulad, a camp does not in terms of its genealogical composition make up a descent segment of that oulad. In camp B are members predominately of two patrilines, in C three, in D two, one of which also constitutes E. The Ali Marduni genealogy in Fig. 4 (p. 57) was collected in the camp of the headman. The descendants of his FaFaFa Mahad Morad number 30 tents within the oulad, the Shahryar nearly an equal number. Yet in the headman's summer camp group of 6 tents, both these quite distant segments were represented, as well as other branches.

In this way, the personnel of an oulad or a section groups itself into a series of camps in terms of the multiple interpersonal bonds that provide an effective basis for solidarity and co-operation. The feature of this organization which is perhaps unusual and interesting is that these politically effective bonds have little or no relation to the rules, or interests, that delimit the aggregate from which the personnel of the camp is drawn. In other words, subdivisions of the oulad are based on criteria entirely different from those that define the oulad itself. None the less they constitute the *de facto* subdivisions of the oulad as a political unit — under prominent leaders who challenge the authority of the headman the camps may constitute politically fissive divisions within the oulad. But they are not segments in terms of the criteria that define oulads — they are not homologous with the oulad. In its political constitution, the oulad is an aggregate of tents under the supervision of a headman; in terms of kinship it is a clearly delimited patrilineal descent group. The camp, which is the primary subdivision of the oulad, is politically structured around one or more influential leaders who by their leadership and influence hold it together as a group; in terms of kinship, it is compound and not clearly delimited.

In purely static and structural terms, this organization may seem unorthodox, but not particularly problematical. Each oulad is a named and clearly delimited unit; it is used by the chief for administrative purposes and has an appointed headman responsible to the chief. Camps are also clearly delimited (by locality); though they move independently of each other, this can be ignored so long as they remain within the limits prescribed by the chief for their oulad.

But any analysis of the system in terms of processes poses problems; particularly with respect to its mechanisms for accommodating the phenomenon of growth and segmentation as a historical process. The difficulty arises from the fact that in the system as described, the social groups at the points of growth are not homologous with the important groupings on higher levels. A camp community which experiences a growth of population does not appear ever to reach a point where it can change into an oulad, since its structure would seem to remain basically different from that of an oulad. A comparison with other forms of unilineal organizations highlights this problem. Thus in a lineage system, the process of growth and segmentation is a part of the lineage process itself: a newborn boy is a potential lineage segment. In other words, at the points of growth, the units formed are homologous with the larger units on higher levels. An internally unsegmented clan, on the other hand, may grow and divide along any

61

politically expedient line, thereby producing two new groups that are homologous with the original undivided whole. But in the Basseri case we have seen no process whereby groups homologous with the oulad can form on lower levels as potentially divisible parts of an as yet undivided oulad. Descent segments within the oulad do not emerge as residential units, nor do they gain any other political relevance through the growth of an oulad; and there is no point at which it becomes feasible, much less advantageous, for ambitious camp leaders to exclude affines and matrikin — their closest supporters — from their camp.

A closer investigation of some of the implications of the processes of camp formation does, I believe, reveal a trend towards the gradual crystallization of patrilineal descent cores in mature camps. But before I embark on the rather complicated argument required to demonstrate this, it is necessary to explore other and simpler explanations. Firstly, the problem is one that will only arise in a situation of consistent over-all population growth, and even then only if there is in fact an optimal size of oulads, and a consequent need for division of large oulads.

These conditions are clearly present. Particularly the Weisi part of the tribe seems in the last 2-3 generations to have increased rapidly. Very old informants tell that in their childhood, whole sections which now contain several oulads used to camp together. Census material suggests a considerable rate of population growth (cf. ch. IX). That this growth should express itself directly in a corresponding growth in the size of oulads, without any multiplication of their numbers, is improbable. Oulads serve as administrative tools for the chief; through the headmen of oulads he regulates migrations and allots pastures. Without an effective organization of this kind, the present size and importance of the tribes in Fars could not be maintained (Barth 1960). In such an administrative scheme, the units to be manipulated clearly have an optimal size — there is a limit to the number of households that can conveniently share undivided pasture rights, and to the number of tents that the chief can control effectively through a single headman. Population growth within oulads therefore creates mounting difficulties in administration which can only be solved by a counterbalancing process of subdivision of large oulads.

That such splitting of oulads has on occasion taken place is implied

62

by the statements of old informants, as cited above. But the Basseri themselves do not regard this as a regular process, but rather as unique historical events, about which they have no detailed information. In other contexts, it is asserted that the schema of oulads and sections is entirely static, and that the groups which exist now have always been. Yet the pattern of subdivision embodied in their own pedigrees and traditions of origin looks like nothing more than the product of a process of growth and segmentation.

There is thus every reason to believe that a multiplication of oulads by segmentation is a continual historical process, though the mechanisms of this process are not self-evident because of the basic difference between the structure of oulads and camps. This difference in structure, however, depends mainly on the genealogical composition of the units, and it is tempting to dismiss the whole problem by positing a process of fabrication of genealogies, not unknown elsewhere, whereby genealogically compound large camps could be given a fictitious agnatic unity. But there is no evidence to support such an explanation; and it leaves a number of features of Basseri organization unexplained. Firstly, there is not the interest in, or the frequent discussion of, pedigrees and genealogies among the Basseri which one would expect if fictitious genealogies were to be produced and disseminated through the population. Furthermore, the pedigrees I collected are full of genealogical material which does *not* harmonize with the *de facto* organizational scheme, as any inspection of the charts in Figs. 3 and 4 will reveal. Discrepancies occur even on the level of oulads between the descent charter and the *de facto* organizational scheme. The clearest case of this which I discovered is in the Labu Musa section. Here, the three oulads of the chief's schema (p. 51) carry the names of their three headmen, and not of any comprehensive descent group. In fact the tripartite division does not correspond to the genealogical division of the Labu Musa by descent, which is into two primary segments, descended from Musa's two sons Yar Mohammed and Geda (Fig. 4 p. 58). Below that level, the Labu Musa operate with respectively seven and five sub-segments — "oulads" in the loose sense of descent group of any kind. Some of these are unrelated in patriline to Musa, but assimilated to the descendants of one or the other of his two sons; and I was unable to obtain agreement on any genealogical schema for his claimed descendants from informants.

However, in the allocation of the tents of the section to each of the three headmen, even recognized patrilineal groupings are cross-cut. Thus, e.g., the Oulad-e-Ali Hemmad of Geda primary descent segment have for at least three generations been under headmen in the line of Jafar, of Yar Mohammed descent, and not with most of their closer patrilineal collaterals, who are under Ahmad. Such discrepancies hardly indicate any prevalence of fictitious genealogies, but rather suggest a failure in the normal processes that produce a fit between politically viable segments and the primary segments in terms of relatively stable genealogical traditions.

Equally, this failure shows that the chief does not have the power arbitrarily to create new oulads and allocate personnel to these new units, even by deferring to the people's own genealogical traditions. This is also shown by the case of the Shahbani oulad of the Abduli. In the census list from 1951 (p. 51), two population figures are given for the Shahbani. This was because the chief had recognized a second headman within the oulad, without succeeding in subdividing it into descent segments — the followings of the two headmen cross-cut in terms of agnatic kinship and could not be defined in terms appropriate for an oulad. In 1958, this condition still prevailed. As in other aspects of his relations with the tribe, the chief relies also in these matters mainly on processes internal to the camp communities, seeking to regulate and guide them rather than to impose arbitrary arrangements.

There thus appear to be no simple mechanisms for the subdivision of Basseri oulads. Yet most sections, such as e. g. the Kolumbei, have been relatively successful at maintaining a correspondence between descent segments and politically recognized oulads, in spite of rapid population growth and probably repeated splitting of units. This suggests the presence of one or several processes, however imperfect, whereby oulads tend over time to become divided into parts that combine factional unity, so as to constitute politically fissive subdivisions, with at least a predominant agnatic unity, whereby they become essentially homologous with oulads, and thus themselves potential oulads through a process of segmentation. Some of the camps depicted in Fig. 2 have these characteristics — a fact that is not satisfactorily explained by the processes of camp formation as they have been described so far.

However, the full implications of those processes have not yet been explored. In analysing camps I indicated the continual restructuring of the camp that takes place as a result of new marriages. Some factors affecting marriage choices are systematic and thus imply a cumulative trend. Secondly, I indicated several forms of mobility in and out of the camp, two of which are important here: a high rate of sedentarization, possibly selective and thereby with a cumulative effect on the structure of the camp group; and a certain frequency of camp exogamy, which because of initial patrilocal residence implies a greater mobility of women than men. These three factors in combination produce a consistent trend towards agnatic consolidation in every camp, in the following manner:

Cumulative changes in camp membership affect the structure of camps. A certain frequency of mobility of whole households between the camps of an oulad or section is indicated, though I was unable to collect reliable systematic data on the subject. However, there is no evidence of any consistent trend dominating such movements, and their effect is thus merely to increase the intermixture of lines within camps. On the other hand, marriages between members of different camps also lead to mobility. Such marriages constitute about 1/3 of the total, and here a consistent trend asserts itself. Since residence is conventionally patrilocal, a majority of extra-camp marriages imply mobility of the woman and not of the man. As a result, a higher proportion of a camp member's patrilateral than matrilateral kinsmen will tend to be present in his camp.

The political importance of close kinship ties to a man's position within his camp encourages systematic efforts to renew such ties in every generation. Primary ties of matrilateral or patrilateral kinship can be "renewed" by the establishment of affinal ties in the succeeding generation; the result is that marriages are directed towards close kinsmen in preference to others, giving a 30 % frequency of cousin marriage. Since there is no normative preference for patrikin, this factor alone produces no trend, but favours all kinsfolk within the camp equally. But as a result of the factor noted above, there tends to be a higher proportion of patrikin, and especially agnates, present within the camp than there are other kinsmen. As a result, there is a statistical trend towards the maintenance of close kinship connections with agnates as against other kinsmen; agnates become more closely knit together by multiple kin ties, and thus tend to remain together in camp.

Through a constant process of sedentarization (cf. chapters VIII & IX), a number of camp members are sloughed off in every generation. Other things being equal, persons belonging to small sibling groups are at a disadvantage in the camp: they have fewer close relatives to lean on, and fail to establish the net of new affinal ties which form the basis of the influence of more fertile families. As a result, natural irregularities in the fertility of different lines are exaggerated, large sibling groups dominating and small ones tending to be eliminated from the camp by sedentarization. Since the bilateral unity of camps depends on criss-crossing intermarriages in every generation between close collaterals, this tendency towards the wholesale removal of whole small sibling groups and infertile lines produces gaps in the network. This gives the camp a tendency to break up into less closely related, inbreeding divisions — each, as we have seen, a potential independent camp with a consistent bias towards the formation of an agnatic core. Rapid growth and fission of genealogically compound camps should thus produce new camps of markedly increased agnatic homogeneity.

For example camp E in Fig. 2 is the product of a very favourable combination of these factors: a prolific patriline succeeded in increasing over three generations. The father of the present camp leader alone had 7 sons and a total in 1958 of 20 male descendants in male line. Because of their size and importance, the central sibling group containing seven brothers attracted two lines of their closest collateral agnates as affines; and together these three groups of brothers formed a large enough group to constitute an independent camp. But it must also be realized that this agnatic unity is far from secure even once it has been established. If rivalry arises, e. g. between the present headman and one of his brothers, each can most rapidly gain strength *vis-à-vis* the other by drawing in their affines, leading to the rapid disappearance of the camp's present character as a relatively pure and complete agnatic descent segment of the larger oulad.

None the less, the above combination of factors clearly produces a trend toward the gradual transformation of genealogically compound camps into camps which maintain their compound and bilateral internal structure, yet constitute essentially discrete and separable

66

patrilineal descent segments of the larger oulad. In spite of the lack of empirical data, one may thus understand the processes involved in the growth and segmentation of oulads, and how a final subdivision becomes possible. The chief, when faced with the administrative necessity to subdivide an oulad which has grown too large, is usually able to place some of its component camps clearly into one or another primary descent segment in terms of the pedigrees of their numerically predominant cores. A basis for subdivision is thus provided by the existing pedigrees, and though pasture rights are allotted to individuals purely in terms of these pedigrees, some whole camps fall clearly into one or another of the new sub-divisions. Many of the politically viable camp units will thus approximate to the form of an oulad sufficiently for fission of the oulad to take place under the chief's supervision. Those camps where distant agnatic collaterals are strongly inter-mixed, however, will be divided in terms of their pasture rights. Where these camps do not predominate, one can imagine a fairly simple weeding-out effect, whereby persons seek membership in strong camps of the new oulad where they have full rights by virtue of their pedigree, as well as good contacts through pre-established matrilateral or affinal ties.

There thus seem to be trends which, in terms of this rather complex argument, make it possible for the chief by careful administration to maintain optimally sized oulads of exclusive agnatic membership in a growing population, in spite of the complete lack of any overt unilineal principle in the process of camp formation. The mechanisms whereby growth and segmentation proceed are not reducible to a single logical principle, as, e. g., in the case of a lineage system, but can none the less be isolated. It is clear, however, that the process of division requires skill and careful planning by the central chief, as well as a general acceptance of his authority. On this background, the full implications of recent Army practices, and some of the reasons for their lack of succeess, are revealed. During the last two years, the Army has adopted the practice of recognizing all ambitious and effective camp leaders as headmen directly responsible for their camp members to the Colonel. But there is no stable way whereby communally held pastures can be allotted systematically to camp units, since there is no way of delimiting camp membership through time to make them permanent groups. The recognition of camps as separate administrative units,

67

instead of as fractions of a larger unit, spells the end of the whole tribal schema for ordering pasture rights and migrations, and leads rapidly to organizational, and thereby economic, collapse.

Other features of Basseri organization are also explained in these terms, perhaps most importantly the basic stability of the genealogical structure above the level of oulads. The nomads of South Persia live in an environment and in circumstances that are extremely variable, where chiefs and Governors come and go, periods of rapid tribal growth are followed by natural and political calamities when a major fraction of the population is swallowed up in sedentary communities, or dispersed, or even perishes. In spite of this, e. g. the names of sections appear to be ancient and to stick with members, even when they are assimilated as refugees in other tribes in distant areas (cf. p. 52). It becomes clear that the genealogical framework on the higher levels, defining sections *(tireh)* and their interrelations, is insulated from most of the processes of petty politics, factionalism and fission, since such processes cannot assert themselves readily on the oulad level or above; while the reorganizing activities of the chief are concentrated primarily at regulating the size and division of oulads. The structure of the larger and more inclusive segments is thus left unaffected, like the calcified limbs of a coral reef; so section names and traditions can serve the tribal population as stable and unchanging anchors of identification under changing circumstances.

Finally, one more aspect of section and oulad organization should be noted: a coalescing process which is the obverse of growth and fission. Between some sections which have not grown very rapidly, a relation of pairing develops. Thus the Farhadi and Zohrabi stand in this special relation to each other, in that their traditional routes and pastures adjoin, and there is a recognized pattern of free intermarriage, while most other groups regard marriage outside the sections as somewhat shameful. In this case, both groups are in a phase of moderate growth and there has been no residential fusion and intermixing of tents, despite affinal connections. Between the Hanai and the Ali Shah Gholi, on the other hand, who are similarly paired and who are both on the decline, the coalescing process has gone further. These groups are very poor and practise a little agriculture, especially in the summer areas. Among them, camps are compounded of both sections (e. g. Fig. 2 camp A); and while the chief still distinguishes between the sections and their estates, they themselves seem no longer to do so. Their little dryland fields are thus intermixed, as are their tents; and the members of one section recognize the authority also of the headman of the other. In periods of decline, the reduced units may thus coalesce and consolidate, by a process far simpler than the process of splitting.

Chapter V

CHIEFTAINSHIP

The scattered and constantly shifting tent camps of the Basseri are held together and welded into a unit by their centralized political system, culminating in the single office of the chief. Though many tribesmen trace descent from common ancestors and thus validate their membership in larger groupings, some camp groups admit divergent origins, while others, outside the tribe, are regarded as close collateral relations. It is the fact of political unity under the Basseri chief which in the eyes of the tribesmen and outsiders alike consitutes them into a single "tribe" in the Persian sense.

The pivotal position then in the whole tribal organization is that of the chief[1]. He is the central, autocratic leader of the tribe. In keeping with the historical forms of centralized leadership found else-where in the Middle East, he is traditionally granted a vast and not clearly delimited field of privilege and command, and power is conceived as emanating *from* him, rather than delegated *to* him by his

---

[1] At the time of my field work, there was legally no longer any chief of the Basseri, since responsibility for the tribe had been assumed by the Iranian Army two years previously. While in the Qashqai area this took the form of dispatching a Colonel to each of the tribal chiefs, whereby the two administer jointly, among the nomadic sections of the Khamseh group the chiefs have been dismissed and sole legal authority vested in the Army, represented by a Colonel. The situation which I shall describe below is thus in a sense a reconstruction of the system as it functioned two years before my visit. Such a reconstruction is meaningful because that system, and not the present one (particularly not in its officially sanctioned form), belongs as an integral part with the other persisting features of Basseri organization which I describe. In almost all its ramifications, chieftain-

71

subjects. In the following I shall attempt to analyse the effective fields and limits of his authority, and the sources from which this authority derives.

Among the nomads of South Persia, there are properly two distinct titles translatable as "chief", namely *Khan* and *Kalantar*. This reflects the organization of politically discrete tribes into larger confederacies, the former led by *kalantars,* subordinate to the *Khan* of their confederacy. But with the wide use of *Khan* as the proper term of polite address for all chiefs, and the political collapse of the confederacies, the title of *kalantar* tends to disappear; and the Basseri chiefs are today both addressed and referred to as *Khan.*

The chiefs of the Basseri belong to a branch of the Mahad Khan oulad of the Kolumbei. An authoritative genealogy including some of the important collateral members of the line is given in Fig. 5, as taken down from Mahad Khan Esvandiari. There is much confusion and disagreement over this genealogy, even with respect to the relationship of the chiefs marked (1) and (2) in the accompanying chart. Other versions were, however, largely simplifications of the one given here, and Mahad Khan was regarded by all as a genealogical/historical authority, who in discussions would convince others of the correctness of his version by marshalling further details of historical tradition.

The ruling chiefs are numbered in the chart from the first *kalantar* remembered by the general population; but there is no evidence that he was in fact the founder of the dynasty. It would appear that only the Weisi part recognized the earlier *kalantars,* and that they and the Ali Mirzai were united under one chief only during the reign of Haji Mohammed Khan. This expansion of the Basseri tribe was continued under Parviz Khan, who added the Ali Ghambari and Ali Shah Gholi,

---

ship also in fact continued at the time of my field work. The change to Army rule had not been accepted by the Basseri tribesmen, who continued to act towards the legally deposed chief as if he were formally in office, while liaison between the Colonel and the tribe was poor. This *de facto* situation was even recognized by the authorities to the extent that when I received my permit from the Army to work among the Basseri, the Commanding General made contact with the "former" Basseri chief to ask him, and not the appropriate Colonel, to make the necessary arrangements with the tribe. The activities and processes I shall describe have thus been observed in the field and serve, to the extent they are sufficient and successful, to maintain the other institutions and organizational form of nomad Basseri society observed and described elsewhere in this study.

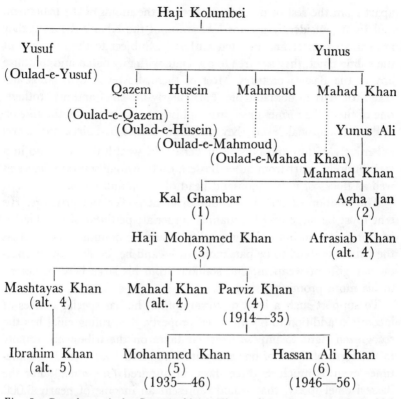

Fig. 5. Genealogy of the Basseri chiefs. The traditionally remembered chiefs are numbered consecutively from Kal Ghambar, and the main rival pretenders of the later chiefs are indicated as alternatives. Only reigning chiefs and important pretenders are shown in the genealogy.

and under Mohammed Khan, who added Il-e-Khas, many Arab splinter groups, and the remains of the Nafar Turks.

Whereas the Kolumbei are generally regarded as forming the core of the Basseri today, it is notable that the dynastic line makes no claim to be the senior line of the Kolumbei. Yusuf is agreed by all to have been senior to Yunus; and Mahad Khan was the youngest of Yunus' sons. In fact it would appear that at least today, the genetic connection between the chiefs and the Kolumbei has no relevance to the legitimacy of the dynasty as chiefs of the Basseri tribe. It is, however, a source of some pride to the Kolumbei.

The chief and his immediate relatives belong in a category entirely

73

apart from the rest of the Basseri, both in the minds of the tribesmen, and to an outsider. They are *Khavanin,* of the Khan's dynasty; they are shown respect and granted authority. Subject to the approval of the ruling chief, they are free to associate with any oulad and to utilize any of the Basseri pastures. Most of them, however, own lands and take little part in nomadic life. Particularly the chief and his brothers, one of them the former chief, are sophisticated members of the *élite* on a Persian national level; they maintain houses in Shiraz and travel extensively within and outside of Persia. In wealth they are also in a class entirely apart from other Basseri, each owning several villages as well as flocks of many thousand head of sheep and goats.

The position of the chief is one of great power and privilege. His tent must be large and his manner imperial; pettiness of any kind is inappropriate to him. His hospitality should be boundless — whereas the tribesmen tend to be parsimonious — and he should provide spectacular gifts of weapons, and stallions from his large herd of horses, to his more prominent subjetcs.

To support such a level of consumption, he has special sources of income in addition to his inherited property. The ruling chief has the recognized right to impose irregular taxes on the tribesmen, usually in the form of a tax of one sheep in a hundred *(sad-o-yek)* or sometimes even as much as three sheep in hundred *(sad-o-seh).* For the Basseri chief today, that would represent an income of nearly 8,000 sheep. In addition, each oulad pays a regular annual tax in clarified butter, and visitors and supplicants to the chief's tent are prone to bring gifts, usually of livestock.

The outstanding feature of the chief's position, however, is his power of decision and autocratic command over his subjects. Decisions governing collectivities among the Basseri are reached either by discussion or by command. I have described above how decisions governing camp groups are made by their members through a lengthy process of discussion and mutual persuasion. Apart from the authority occasionally exercised by the head of a household within his own tent, this is the only type of decision-making process in which the common Basseri participates. The right to command, to make decisions on behalf of persons in other tents than one's own, is a strictly chiefly prerogative. The monopolization by the chief of the right to command is a fundamental abstract principle of Basseri social structure. This

74

idea was clearly expressed by informants, who where perhaps particularly aware of the chief's special position because of the disturbance caused by his formal deposition. All contemporary ills were explained by the resulting lack of a centralized coercive authority — the tribe without its chief was compared to a flock without its shepherd and a car without its driver. When I once tried to make some limited arrangements involving the movements of the camp in which I lived, stating that I would assume full responsibility for these arrangements, I was met with the objection that I was behaving like a chief and infringing on his rights.

However, though one may characterize the political organization of the Basseri by the abstracted principle of monopolization of coercive authority by the chief, such a formulation has in itself little meaning. One needs to have a picture of the organization in terms of how it maintains itself, and this is not given by distilling and abstracting its structural principle, even when the tribesmen themselves are aware of that principle. An analysis of the political organization calls for an analysis of the processes whereby the powers of the chief are exercised and defended. In the following I shall attempt to make such an analysis, first by describing the administrative apparatus at the chief's disposal and the fields in which his authority is exercised, and then by analysing his sources of power *vis-à-vis* the tribesmen, whereby his position of command is maintained.

The formal apparatus of the chief's administration is quite simple — rather surprisingly so in view of the difficulties of communication, and the apparent autocratic powers he exercises. Each oulad is, as we have seen, under a headman *(katkhoda),* of which there were properly 32 in the Basseri tribe at the time of the chief's deposition. These headmen act as the communicating links between their oulads and the chief when the chief is not himself present in their camp; but it is characteristic that the headmen do not represent a separate echelon of command: wherever his subjects are present, the chief deals directly with them and never through their headman, and in his decisions he does not take the opinion of the headman into particular account. All Basseri are equal in their direct relation of subordination to the chief, who at any time may give any person an order which the latter must obey without regard to any pre-established organizational pattern. The hierarchy of organization consists of chains of *communication* from the central chief to all his scattered subjects, not of chains of *command* — which is another way of describing the monopolization of coercive authority noted above.

Associated with the chief is a special section of the tribe, the Darbar, known among most other tribes in Fars as the Amaleh. They travel with the chief and camp with him, and are without a formal headman. Among the members of the Darbar are found a personal valet, a master of the stores, a groom for the chief's riding horses, a scribe, and a hunting-and-drinking companion *cum* court jester. These offices were for explanatory purposes characterized by the common descriptive Persian terms for such offices; but since each is unique and personal in the tribe, the names of the office-holders were otherwise always used, and not their titles. Such office-holders, just like other members of the Darbar, each have their own flocks and tents and property, so in the absence of the chief the Darbar is indistinguishable from any other oulad.

In addition to these officers, the chief also has special contracts with persons who tend his flocks. At the time of my visit, the chief's sheep and goats were divided on several hands, one of them in the Darbar, his camels were herded by another member of the Darbar, while a herd of several hundred horses, predominantly mares and foals, was kept by some persons in a camp of the Jouchin.

The fields in which the chief regularly exercises authority, i. e. his main functions for the tribe, may be grouped in three: allotting pastures and co-ordinating the migrations of the tribe; settling the disputes that are brought to him; and representing the tribe or any of its members in politically important dealings with sedentary authorities.

It is mainly the co-ordination of tribal migrations that requires any ramifying administrative organization at all. The units involved in this are oulads, and orders regarding their movements pass mainly through the headmen, sometimes with the addition of a chief's representative and observer *(ma'umur)* assigned to each headman. These representatives were mainly drawn from the Darbar, and were particularly important some years ago, following the sweeping re-organization of migration routes and the distribution of pastures instituted by the last chief on his accession. Communications from the chief are relayed by word of mouth via messengers — a service to which any Basseri may be deputed — while much general information reaches the chief via the many visitors to his tent.

In the small and closely knit communities that constitute camps, most matters of law are governed by custom and compromise and regulated by diffuse sanctions. Where disputes cannot be settled informally, recourse may be had to the chief, who alone constitutes the only "court" in the tribal system. The chief is not bound by custom or precedent in his decision — the cases that are brought before him are precisely such as cannot be mediated within the framework of tradition, for reasons of their subject, or the personalities involved. Nor is he expected to give judgement according to the Shariat, which he does not claim to know and which runs clearly counter to important fields of custom. Quite explicitly, he is expected to make the decision which he feels is "best for the tribe" — he is expected to exercise his privileged arbitrary authority within a very wide area of free grace, unhampered by considerations of individual justice as derived from rules. Only in disputes over the division of an inheritance does he restrict his autocratic power — such cases he frequently refers for decision to a religious judge in a sedentary community.

The chief's "court" hearings are singularly lacking in formality. Any direction by the chief is an order, any definite statement is a decision, whether expressed as an aside in a conversation, or while washing his hands or taking his meal. Ceremony and pomp are only emphasized in "foreign" relations *vis-à-vis* non-Basseri visitors, particularly other chiefs and prominent men of the sedentary society.

Perhaps the chief's most important function is to represent the tribe in its relations with the Iranian administration, and in conflicts with sedentary communities or persons. This touches on a very fundamental problem in the organization of "plural" societies — societies composed of ethnically distinct groups in close interdependence in some fields of activity, while dissimilar and unconnected in other aspects of their social life. Where persons or groups belonging to such different parts of a plural society meet, there must be mechanisms mediating the relationship between them — within the limited situation of their interaction, they must be "comparable" in some appropriate framework. Usually, as in the case where the concept of plural society was first developed (Furnivall 1944), this situation is the market place, where people meet as buyers and sellers, producers and consumers,

77

and are equally subject to the "terms of trade" regardless of the differences in their backgrounds. So also in Fars, where the nomad meets the villager in economic transaction, the interaction is direct and relatively uncomplicated, governed by supply and demand in a monetary exchange system (cf. pp. 98 ff.).

In the relations between groups of tribesmen and the organs of government, or where conflicts between a nomad and a sedentary are made the subject of judicial procedure, however, the situation is far more complex. Let us discuss the latter example first.

We have seen how a conflict between two Basseri nomads is settled, firstly by appeal to public opinion and the use of diffuse sanctions within the camp, and, if these fail, by the arbitrary decision of the chief. The persons or groups involved in such conflicts are homologous and fully comparable; their choices are subject to the same restrictions and actions directed against them have similar consequences for both parties.

Similarly, where two farmers in sedentary communities come into conflict, their positions are comparable: they are subject to the same public opinion, may appeal to the same or equivalent village headmen, or can go to the court of the subdistrict or district in which they live.

When, on the other hand, a conflict arises between a nomad and a farmer, e. g. because the former's herd has damaged the latter's crops, the position is different, and the problem of equivalence and comparability arises. In the case of the Basseri, this is not because of an extreme ethnic contrast — the language, religion, and major aspects of custom are shared. But pastoral nomadism by its technical requirements affects the position of the nomad and restricts the possible range of his actions in very determinate ways, which are very different from the restrictions implied by farming. The farmer's community and land are stationary; though his crops require attention, they readily survive a week's neglect. The nomad camp must move, for the sake of the herds; so to remain a member of his community the nomad can at most linger one or two days in any one locality. His property cannot be left in the charge of "neighbours", since it requires many hours of work each day to move it with the camp; his flocks are held together only by his constant shepherding, so his whole means of livelihood will be lost by a single day's neglect.

In other words, the opponents in a conflict between a nomad and a farmer cannot maintain contact for long; the difference in their modes of life precludes all the activities usually associated with mediation and the settlement of conflicts. Left to their own devices they can only mobilize their own communities and fight it out — and the prevalence of fortified villages in Southern Fars bears evidence to the frequency of this resort in the past, and its occasional practice today.

Alternatively, the farmer may take his grievance to the local court. But there the nomad cannot without great hardship even plead his case; while the farmer can readily sit for a week on the courthouse doorstep, the nomad is in practice unable to comply even with a court summons. If he succeeds in interesting the court at all, the farmer can thus mobilize a vast and powerful bureaucratic apparatus, the rules of which the nomad, because of his pastoral mode of life, is forced to break. On the other hand, internal tribal judicial mechanisms are equally unsuited for the farmer.

Between nomad and sedentary there are thus no mechanisms on the level of local communities for the regulation of social relations by law, and for the resolution of conflicts by other means than by violence; nor would it seem possible to develop other than very imperfect mechanisms on that level. A workable mechanism can only be achieved by channelling such conflicts through administrative superstructures which bridge this difference by transforming the interests and the social units concerned to a point where they become comparable and thus able to communicate.

Our primary interest here lies with the tribal side of this bridge. It is provided by the institution of centralized chieftainship. Whereas the common tribesmen from a sedentary point of view are elusive and irresponsible, the chief of a tribe is a known and responsible entity. It is in his interest to maintain stable and peaceful relations with the centres of power in sedentary society; and this he can do because he has the domestic staff that frees him from all pastoral and household duties. Where the common tribesman's relations with sedentary society are largely unstable and passing, his are continuous and permanent. His whereabouts in an area are always known, at least roughly; and since he maintains a house in Shiraz, he has a "permanent address". This places him on a par with the landowning *élite* of sedentary society, who also keep houses in Shiraz, but are occasionally, although less frequently, absent on tour of their villages. Where conflicts arise between tribesman and villager, the chief can represent the interests of his tribe, just as the landowner or local administrator can represent that of the villagers. They can meet as equals before the Provincial Governor, or in court, or directly. The two parties have thus on this level become comparable, and their conflicting interests amenable to negotiation and settlement in a political or a legal framework. Though the chief's influence in the provincial capital in large part derives from his *de facto* power as leader of a powerful tribe, the important fact here is that he is acceptable as a person and as an equal of the local *élite* because he is like them — he shares their diacritical symbols and can participate in their activities.

The chief's role in mediating relations with the sedentary society, in protecting the nomadic herders' interests *vis-à-vis* the often formidable and always confusing organizations that structure parts of their environment and encroach on their life, is correlated with a strong feeling of respect and dependence among the tribesmen. They explicitly recognize that without their chief they would be helpless in a number of recurring situations. Together with the chief's important role in directing the migrations and settling internal disputes, this might constitute a functional "explanation" of the great authority of the chief. However, the persistence of an institution is not exhaustively explained by a demonstration of its usefulness. The position of autocratic authority occupied by the Basseri chief can only be successfully maintained and defended if it is supported by enough coercive power to enforce discipline and suppress opposition from below, no matter how opportunistic and short-sighted such opposition may be. The fact that many tribesmen sooner or later in the course of their lifetime find themselves in a position where they desperately need the help of their chief cannot in itself serve him as a source of such power. The apparently poor development of formal groupings supporting the chief's coercive authority is thus surprising; and the Basseri political system requires further analysis, in terms of the political balance between its constituent groups, to be understood.

This means looking at the political system in its complete form as the "power household" of the tribe. In these terms, positions of authority can only be stable if the incumbent of such a position is able to mobilize enough force to counter any group that can form

within the system to question his authority. The coercive requirements of the chief are thus not directly proportional to the extent of
his authority, but depend on the political constitution of his subjects,
on the patterns of leadership and organization not directly under his
control.

We must therefore return to the camps, as the basic spontaneous
political groupings in Basseri society, and investigate their pattern
of leadership and their possible interconnections from this point of
view. As shown in the description of camps (pp. 26 ff.), the camp
leader depends on influence for his position of leadership, and to
prevent the fragmentation of his camp he is continually concerned to
achieve uninamity, without access to coercive means. In this process,
there is no crystallization of political "parties", since numbers are
irrelevant: if *one* man remains adamant, the remainder of the camp
does not constitute a majority party which can impose its decision on
the group as a whole — there is no "majority" in terms of coercive
power. The techniques of camp leadership are thus, as emphasized,
those of compromise, persuasion, and a keen awareness of the drift
of group opinion.

Clearly, this kind of leader can never serve as the rallying point of
a strong faction or party; he is sensitive to all external as well as
internal pressures and seeks to resolve them by accommodating them
all, and by avoiding partisan commitments. Nor does any pattern of
alignment of whole camps into two or more blocs develop, partly for
this same reason, partly because of the prevailing suspicions and lack
of intercommunication which isolate Basseri camps from one another.
They are furthermore in a competitive relation to one another, since
all camps by their presence restrict each other in the utilization of
pastures and water.

The political subjects of the chief are thus organized in small,
mutually hostile, and weakly led groups, each striving to maintain
internal harmony and unanimity without coercive means. These are
the only organized groups, and the only kind of leaders, within the
Basseri system which can challenge the chief's authority and with
which he must be able to deal. The poor development of centrally
controlled coercive means reflects this impotence of any potential
opposition. In most situations, camps and their leaders can be controlled merely by assertive and definitive orders from the chief; the

81

mere pressure of such statements, backed by the chief's influence, prevents any disagreements from becoming explicit. Insubordination usually takes the form of verbal compliance with an order or instruction, but failure to execute it in practice; the sanction by which this is discouraged and punished is verbal abuse, and in more serious cases, corporal punishment. Orders are given in a form so that a particular person is responsible for their execution; and failure is punished unless it is reported and depends on some other person's refusal to comply. Thus no power is delegated even to persons who have duties and responsibilities foisted on them, except that power implicit in the right to report cases of resistance to the chief. Failure to execute an order from the chief can thus always be traced to one particular individual, who becomes liable to punishment.

Corporal punishment takes place in the presence of the chief and is specified by him — usually in the form of a certain number of strokes with a stout pole. Such punishment is painful and in more severe cases dangerous. The beating is not performed by any special category of functionary — any bystander who is a member of the tribe may be ordered to do it. The only collective punishment employed is a fine, levied as an extra tithe on the flocks belonging to the members of an oulad or section who are held collectively responsible for a mis-deed, such as trespassing on the pasture rights of others. The collection of such fines is made the duty of a person unconnected with the group concerned — usually a member of the Darbar.

These characteristic features of the position of the Basseri chief are also apparent in the rules and practices in connection with succession. All close agnates of a chief are his potential successors, though usually only a few of them emerge as pretenders upon his death. Candidacy is by announcement, or rather assumption, since it is also marked by the person beginning to exercise a chief's authority; there is no previous appointment of an heir apparent, though sometimes one son clearly points himself out as the one most likely to succeed.

As shown above, the Basseri political system does not produce strong opposed factions; so on the death of a chief, his potential successors stand without crystallized followings in the tribe, apart from their small retinue of personal servants and shepherds. Nor can the pretenders "seize the reins of government", since there is no formal adminstrative apparatus, the control of which might put a pretender in a position where he could effectively rule the tribe. Without social organs of an importance and dignity comparable to chieftaincy, there is not even any formal appointment or investiture of the successful pretender and *de facto* ruler — in a sense, he remains only *de facto* until he dies or is overthrown.

Almost at every point of succession, and occasionally in between, there appear among the Basseri to have been periods of confusion, when several "chiefs" have ruled simultaneously and vied for control of the tribe. The outlines of these internal dynastic turmoils are shown in Fig. 5 (p. 73). The last case of succession seems to have passed relatively unchallenged, and was unusual in that it involved a voluntary abdication, by Mohammed Khan, under strong external as well as internal pressure, in favour of his younger brother Hassan Ali Khan, who had always supported Mohammed Khan during his reign. The accession of Mohammed Khan, on the other hand, was far from untroubled. Though he was only 18 years old at the time of his father's death, he had exercised authority almost to the point of usurping his father's position for several years. Yet his cousin Ibrahim declared himself Khan and apparently exercised authority quite as successfully as Mohammed Khan for at least 6 months at the beginning of Mohammed Khan's rule, and again for a period while the latter was a prisoner of the Qashqai. The preceding rule of Parviz Khan was challenged several times by Parviz's brothers, and on his accession there was a period of confusion when not only they, but also Afrasiab Khan of a collateral line of the dynasty (FaFaBrSo of Parviz Khan) all tried to win control of the tribe. Similar rivalries appear to have taken place at previous points of succession, and to be common also in neighboring tribes.

The different informants' memories from these periods following the death of a chief, or a challenge to his authority, are highly contradictory and reflect the prevailing confusion at such times. Apparently, the several chiefs with their entourages move independently in the tribe, and each assert their authority, without building up a following of supporters in the tribe proper. The tribesmen respect all members of the dynasty, and comply with the orders of the chief's collaterals even in periods of stable rule. In periods of rivalry, they merely obey the orders last received, or from whichever pretender is present. Their impressions from such periods are thus various, depending on the contacts which their camp happened to have with different pretenders.

The clarification of successional disputes is a gradual process, and depends on the effects of the same kinds of control as those by which a ruling chief limits the authority of his dynastic collaterals. Through his stronger and more effective exercise of authority, one of the pretenders increasingly points himself out as the natural leader. In the words of the Basseri themselves, "the horse feels the rider's thigh" — the tribesmen sense and respond to willpower and assurance. Though the authority of other pretenders may not be directly challenged by the common tribesmen, people start dragging their feet and fail to act on the orders of other pretenders than one, until one day the whole edifice of administrative decisions and imperious manner built up by the unsuccessful pretender collapses, and nobody listens to him any more. Throughout such periods of confusion, the threat of assassination by the paid agent of a rival hangs over every pretender — increasingly so as his authority in the tribe wanes — so frequently the unsuccessful pretenders fear for their lives and escape to neighbouring, opposed tribes when they feel that the current runs against them. At a later point, when the new ruler feels secure in his position, they may be permitted to return and re-establish themselves as respectable members of the dynasty, as has, e. g., Mahad Khan, the uncle of the present chief (Fig. 5). Since few of the commoners take sides in the successional disputes, only a handful of followers accompany their chief in exile, or need to flee in the event of his death[1]. Defections from the tribe by larger groups of commoners are caused rather by the ruthlessnes of strong chiefs, and thus occur during stable periods of rule, not as a sequel to successional disputes.

A chief thus achieves his position of authority by the same means as he maintains it: by its effective and continuous exercise, supported by the threat of corporal punishment of subordinates and assassination of competitors. Since in these activities he is independent of any formalized administrative machinery, his authority is not very closely delimited in the tribe — it extends to a variety of fields and gives him

---

[1] In the Darbar are found the descendants of a few such refugees from the Qashqai Amaleh who left upon the death of Chengish Khan, supposedly poisoned by his Br. and successor Saulat-e-Daulat, the father of Nasr Khan, who is the contemporary chief of the Qashqai.

great personal latitude, or area of "free grace". Nor is it strictly delimited to a determinate social group. Nothing in the organization precludes a chief of strong will and personality from exercising authority over the subjects of another chief, if the two tribes have friendly relations. Unless a commoner is in a structural position which permits him to adopt a consistently hostile or violent attitude to a chief, he must show deference and thus becomes liable to that chief's influence and authority. Between friendly tribes, a division of authority over their component camps can thus only be maintained by a balanced opposition of the power centres represented by the chiefs themselves. In frequent cases, therefore, one chief is able to extend his sphere of control and encroach on, or even usurp, the authority of another. Among the Basseri, Mohammed Khan succeeded in this fashion in extending his authority over the Nafar Turkish-speaking tribe, only 40 years ago as numerous as the whole Basseri. Under the weak chief Yusuf Beg Nafar, this tribe experienced a decline, and when Mohammed Khan started directing the migrations of the remaining sections, Yusuf Beg was unable to assert any effective contrary authority, and the Nafar came under the sway of the Basseri chief.

The effects of this process of encroachment and usurpation of authority by one chief over the subjects of another are further magnified by the response it calls forth in the nomad population at large. Camps, oulads and sections seek out the strong chief and submit to him; from him they obtain better protection and by him their interests are best safeguarded. It was noted earlier that a "tribe" among South Persian nomads is a political concept; its unity is not ethnic, but depends on its allegiance to a chief. The processes whereby ethnic complexity persists in the tribes, and whereby rapid changes in their relative and absolute sizes take place, can now be better understood. Any imbalance between tribes in the effectiveness of centralized authority stimulates an extension of the stronger centre's claims to authority, and a voluntary flow of commoners from the weaker to the stronger centre.

Such movements are reversible and ever-changing, reflecting the balance of the moment. The Basseri, like most other tribes, have experienced both ups and downs. They were an independent, though relatively small tribe composed mainly of Ali Mirzai sections in the time of Nasr-ud-Din Shah (1848-96)[1]. In the next 20 years, there was a collapse of ordered government in the provinces, related to the constitutional struggles in Teheran; and in this period the Arab tribes became more powerful, dominating the Basseri and ruling many of its sections[1]. Thus the Shaibani Khans of the Arabs assumed control of the Labu Musa and the Abduli (under Khan Baz Khan), and the Ali Ghambari (under his son Asgar Khan)[2]. During the chieftaincy of Haji Mohammed Khan (Fig. 5) the balance was reversed. His son Parviz Khan further married a daughter of the Shaibanis, as did also his son, Mohammed Khan. This close kinship connection with the Shaibani Khans facilitated the assumption of authority by the Basseri Khans over a number of sections of Shaibani subjects, not only those of Basseri origin but also increasingly those of Arab stock. Before his abdication Mohammed Khan thus had direct or indirect control over about half the Arab tribes — those traditionally under Shaibani Khans — as well as a few splinters (e. g. the Safari) from groups traditionally under the other main Arab dynasty, the Jabbare. Present political circumstances, however, prevent the Basseri chief from exercising and consolidating this control.

The authority structure of the nomad camp and tribe also influences the form of the highest level of tribal organization: the confederacy. Though the Khamseh confederacy to which the Basseri belong is now practically defunct, it has till recently been of great importance, and requires some description.

The Khamseh (Arabic: "five together") contains five distinct tribes: the Arabs of Fars, under a medley of large and small chiefs, the Turk tribes of Ainalu, Baharlu, and Nafar, and the Persian-speaking tribe of Basseri. The confederacy is recent, only 90-100 yeras old, and its origin must be traced, not to any of the constituting nomad tribes, but to the bazaars and governmental palaces of Shiraz.

The founders and rulers of the Khamseh confederacy are the Ghavam family[3]. This family traces its origin from a merchant by the name Mohammed, who came to Shiraz from Kazvin, though his

---

[1] Both statements according to Ghavam-ul-Mulk, cf. p. 88.

[2] According to Asad Khan, the son of Asgar Khan.

[3] This account is based, except where otherwise stated, on information gathered during an interview I had with Ibrahim Ghavam-ul-Mulk, as well as on various accounts by Basseri informants.

86

Mohammed

Mahmoud

Mohammed Hashem

Haji Ibrahim
Etemad-at-Dowleh

Ali Akbar
Ghavam-ul-Mulk

Ali Mohammed
Ghavam-ul-Mulk

Mohammed Reza
Ghavam-ul-Mulk

Habibullah
Ghavam-ul-Mulk

Ibrahim
Ghavam-ul-Mulk

Fig. 6. The heads of the Ghavam family from its founding to the present.

family supposedly was Shirazi by origin. His son Mahmoud became very prosperous, mainly from profits on trade through the southern ports of Kharak and Bandar Abbas, successors to the once fabulous Hormuz; and he thus laid the foundations for the family's great wealth, as well as their connections with the tribes in the South. His grandson, Haji Ibrahim, achieved political prominence as Minister of State to Karim Khan Zand and later to the first Qajars; in 1802 (Sykes 1921: 285) he was executed and the whole family exterminated by Fath Ali Shah, with the exception of one young son, Ali Akbar, who escaped and later returned and claimed his inheritance. The family quickly regained its political prominence in Shiraz, taking the title Ghavam-ul-Mulk. The building of the crystal palace which is an imposing sign of their wealth and prominence, and still the headquarters of the family, was started by Ali Mohammed and completed by his son.

As erstwhile Governors of Fars the Ghavam came into conflict with the increasingly important and powerful Qashqai confederacy; and it was as a counter-weight to the Qashqai, as well as to protect his caravans to and from the southern ports, that Ali Mohammed Ghavam-ul-Mulk caused the Khamseh confederacy to be formed, with himself as its chief.

For four generations, till Ibrahim Khan's deposition by Reza Shah in the early 30's, the Ghavam family of merchants thus served as leaders of one of the largest nomad confederacies of South Persia. Details of this organization are now difficult to unearth; but some of its general outlines are clear. The confederacy seems to have been without any special administrative apparatus, Ghavam visiting separate chiefs or calling them together in *ad hoc* meetings, and dealing directly and personally with them. The allegiance of the tribal chiefs was obtained by gifts of arms, of great importance to the receiving chiefs, and by the important services Ghavam could provide as a sponsor and protector of the tribes' interests *vis-à-vis* the Shah's government. Yet their allegiance was never secure, and he often had to resort to force to reduce various tribes or parts of tribes to submission, either by the seizure and execution of chiefs, or by relatively large-scale punitive expeditions. Though the Khamseh, according to Ghavam's estimate, numbered around 16,000-17,000 tents 50 years ago, they could not be readily mobilized in his support. Thus in the operations during the First World War, when Ghavam supported the British, the Khamseh supplied only a variable and relatively small fraction of the forces at his disposal (Sykes 1921: II, pp. 480, 503, 512).

The precariousness of the unity of the Khamseh confederacy, and of its control by the Ghavams, is suggested by the last case of succession, in 1916, which happened to take place in a Basseri camp in the presence of several of my informants. Habibullah Ghavam-ul-Mulk was travelling toward Shiraz at the time and staying with the recently acceded Parviz Khan of the Basseri when he fell from his horse during hunting and died. The fact of his death, however, was kept secret; he was reported to be ill while the body was kept in a tent under guard of his personal servants and a message was sent to Shiraz for his son Ibrahim to proceed to the spot; and not until the son had established himself among the nomad chiefs was the death of his father revealed.

In view of this weak point in the organization, connected with succession, the use of the name "Ghavam" is interesting, as it represents a pattern to my knowledge unique in the area. Not only is it used as a surname; without modifying personal names it is universally used as a term of reference and address to the ruling head of the Ghavam family. Even while giving the account of succession above, in the words of the tribesmen it was "Ghavam" who fell from his horse and "Ghavam" who announced his father's death. The continuity produced by this, in a situation where other persons do not even have surnames, is striking. Perhaps significant is the fact that when Ghavam decided to encourage and depend on the Basseri tribe, he bestowed the name "Zarghami" on Parviz Khan and his successors — a name which shows a tendency to be passed on and used in the same manner.

The development of a confederacy thus seems to be only a further elaboration of the pattern of centralized authority represented by the chiefs, and did not among the Khamseh depend on other sources of authority or elaborate any important organizational patterns of its own. It remained as a superstructure on the system, which could be fairly easily shattered by external intervension without greatly disturbing the fabric of tribal organization.

The main argument of this chapter might now be summarized. I have tried to analyse some of the political processes that play a part in producing the form of centralized organization found among the Basseri nomads. The resultant picture lacks the unity of a conventional "structural" description. This is inevitable, since phenomena historically unconnected and logically of different order appear to combine to produce this system.

Throughout the analysis, I have emphasized the relevance of certain aspects of the total environment in which the Basseri live, and their pastoral form of subsistence, to their forms of organization. Important in this chapter has been the fact that the Basseri travel thinly dispersed over areas with large sedentary populations entirely unconnected to the tribal organization. These towns and villages have for thousands of years been under some kind of centralized, bureaucratic administration — one in which authority is monopolized by a restric-

89

ted class, vesting great arbitrary powers in some few persons. Any political body in South Persia, even if pastoral and nomadic, must deal with these persons by having a regular point of articulation with the sedentary hierarchy of authorities.

But there is also power flowing from other sources — here, from collectivities of free tribesmen, who for one thing constitute a mobile, ready-made cavalry force. My further point is that as a correlate to their pastoral adaptation, the communities in which these nomad tribesmen live have a composition and organization which militates against the emergence of strong leaders within camps.

This opens a niche for the political figure we have been concerned to analyse here: the omnipotent Khan or chief. Through him, as a bridge of communication, the nomads' relations with sedentary society may be mediated. By being the leader of tribesmen, a power factor in the province, he can become a member of the privileged urban *élite*, and is thus able to defend the interests of the tribe within the sedentary hierarchy of authority, from a vantage point which is unattainable to any active pastoralist. The tribal communities, by accepting such leadership, can obtain substantial benefits. But since they lack strong leaders on the level of their own communities, they lack mechanisms for delimiting and containing the powers of leaders on higher levels of tribal organization; and they thus become subjects of the chief on terms of autocratic dominance/submission. In the extreme case, as we saw in the Khamseh development, this power niche may even be invaded not from the tribes, but from the Persian side of the system, by a far-seeing city financier.

Chapter VI

ATTACHED GYPSY TRIBE

To complete the picture of the Basseri tribe mention should be made of a small attached group of tinkers and smiths, of a people dispersed throughout Persia and known in the South mainly under the names *Ghorbati* or *Kowli*. A distinction of meaning is sometimes made between these two terms, *Kowli* being more free-wandering, trading in various types of easily transportable goods, and without political patrons, like the Gypsies of North and Central Europe; while the groups attached to South Persian tribes prefer to be known as *Ghorbati*.

The *Ghorbati* speak a language or jargon of their own (cf. J.R.A.I. 1902: 344-52), widely distributed in Persia; and they are strongly marked off as a special ethnic group by their customs and mode of life. In the Basseri tribe they constitute a guest population of 50-60 tents, each occupied by an elementary family. They are under the protection of the Basseri chief, and are divided into two camps, each with its own headman. These relatively large camps remain together throughout most of the year, especially during the main periods of migration.

Ghorbati camps are readily recognizable by their characteristic tents. In the camp I visited, only the headman had a tent of usual Basseri construction, while the other families live in tents made of a single cloth, pegged down in all four corners. Towards the front the cloth is held up by two short poles, slanting slightly laterally and forming the sides of the central opening which serves as the entrance and is no more than c. 1.5 m high. Further towards the back, a single, centrally placed T-shaped pole c. 1.2 m high supports the roof.

The migratory cycle of the Ghorbatis differs somewhat from that of their hosts. The winter they spend in the Basseri Garmsir, but they mostly reside with permanent partners, or "friends", in the sedentary villages. In spring they migrate northward with the tribe, but in summer generally travel on, dispersing on trade beyond Isfahan towards Teheran, and sometimes even onward to Khorasan. In the autumn they rejoin the Basseri and migrate with them to the winter areas again.

They keep donkeys and some few horses, in which they trade; but they have no sheep or goats. Their subsistence depends mainly on their smithery. Before each tent stands the anvil of the husband, which is home-made like all the other smithing tools. The men are continually occupied in producing horse-shoes, spindle-whorls, sheep-shears, and other iron tools; they also repair such tools and equipment, and produce and repair pots and pans, as well as scrubbing and polishing any metal utensil for a small fee. They are familiar with techniques for casting iron, and for hardening iron to steel; but they know nothing of iron smelting, even from bog ore, so they depend on the bazaar for their supply of raw iron. Ghorbati men and women also produce woven reed mats, large sieves of perforated sheets of gut, brooms, and small wooden implements.

In part such items are made at the request of nomads in the camps with which they seek contact; but mostly they are offered ready-made for sale by bands of women who visit the different camps, begging and carrying news as well as selling. Payment is in cash or in kind, and is the subject of much haggling.

The Ghorbatis form a despised pariah group; there is no kinship and little communication between them and the nomads. They are predominately endogamous, though occasionally intermarrying with poor families in the villages of the Basseri summer pastures.

Their only importance to the nomads derives from their usefulness as an alternative source of supply of the utensils and equipment enumerated above, especially where bazaars are far away, or for other reasons inaccessible. Their formal attachment as clients of the Basseri chief provides a guarantee of, and consequently a greater stability in, their relations with the tribesmen. This serves a useful function mainly in reducing the mutual distrust and suspicion between the Ghorbatis and the pastoralists who constitute a major part of their market.

Chapter VII

EXTERNAL RELATIONS

While the description so far has centred on social relations within the Basseri population, by which it is organized into a tribe, a number of interrelations have also been noted between Basseri of various statuses, and persons outside the tribal system. These are vitally important to the Basseri, and are highly relevant to the forms of relationships within the tribe, as was apparent particularly in the analysis of the position of the chief. Logically, these relations to persons outside the tribe are of two main kinds: *corporate* relations, whereby the tribe as a unit, or corporate sections of it, are related to groups and statuses outside the tribe, and *individual* relations, whereby numerous tribesmen establish independent contacts with persons outside the tribe, and thus collectively produce a mesh of ties between the tribe and its social environment.

External relations of the corporate kind seem always to involve the whole tribe as a unit, and are in the main political. Those within the framework of the Khamseh confederacy, with traditionally friendly tribes, have already been touched on, and the chief's role in mediating them has been described.

Stable relations with tribes outside the Khamseh confederacy are also mediated by the chief. This is not because common tribesmen lack opportunities for establishing such relations. Most of the camps moving in the main Basseri channel of migration (cf. Barth 1960) are Khamseh, while the Qashqai mostly travel further west; but for about 100 miles of their route, the Basseri tend to become intermixed with Shishbeluki and some other Qashqai groups, while throughout their route in the spring they follow on the heels of, and in the autumn

93

are in turn followed by, the Kurdshuli tribe, which is at present un-connected with either of the big confederacies. There are thus ample opportunities for making contact with these non-Khamseh tribes — in fact, however, the camps entirely avoid each other, and even when natural conditions force them close together for one stage, no social advances are made. The only contacts that a common tribesman makes with members of hostile tribes are when he is searching for lost livestock in foreign areas or in stretches of country occupied at the time by foreign camps. These searches are considered dangerous by the Basseri; and the co-operation of foreign tribesmen is only obtained by sizable offers of payment for information *(moshteluq)*, to a value of ¼ to ⅓ of the lost animals.

Contacts between the chiefs of such hostile tribes are more frequent, and are considered to be of great political importance[1]. Their purpose is mainly to negotiate agreements on the division of pastures and other resources, and to limit inter-tribal violence so as to avoid a situation of complete anarchy destructive to the interests of all the pastoral tribes. Such "state visits" are the occasion for much formality and conspicuous consumption and considerable stereotyped rivalry.

It is regarded as important on such occasions to supply lavish hospitality. Enormous traditional guest tents (5 by 10 by 4 metres) decked with tassels and banners are erected, as well as large modern canvas tents; sheep and pilau and tea are cooked in separate kitchen tents by servants and members of the Darbar; there is music and dancing by women and by men, and horse-racing and target practice. The largest and best carpets are brought out, and wealth in other handicraft products exhibited. Such feasts are regarded by the tribes-men as the high points in nomadic life.

Various opportunities are offered for the expression of rivalry and claims to status by guest and host. As we passed the sites of such past meetings, members of the Darbar would point them out and cite sig-nificant incidents — how in one place, Mohammed Khan had kept Nasr Khan of the Qashqai waiting for two hours after his arrival,

---

[1] Since the chief was not formally active in these matters during my fieldwork, I have no first-hand observations on the subject. The following is based on implicit and explicit information from the tribesmen and the chief, and on the observation of the arrangements during visits to the chief of groups of prominent private individuals.

while he himself remained in his private tent with his family; how in a narrow gorge where he was driving a jeep he refused to give way on meeting Nasr Khan, and forced him to back and let the Basseri chief by, etc. Skill in hunting, by the chief or by his close companions, is also an important field of rivalry. Meetings between chiefs are the occasion for large communal hunts, either for gazelles by large groups of mounted men, or for mountain sheep and goats which are driven into range by picket lines composed of the host tribe. Stories are told of challenges to fell beasts at great distances, and the feats of marksmanship performed.

Meetings between chiefs may take place in spite of active hostility in the border zone between the two tribes. Thus in the period of the two visits by Nasr Khan cited above, Mohammed Khan was attempting to expand the area under his control by buying some villages in the mountain area, owned by third parties but located accross the border in the traditional pasture areas of the Qashqai. Because of threats from the Qashqai chief, the completed purchase of three of these villages was cancelled, while one which Mohammed Khan retained was looted and burned, its tenants prevented by Qashqai tribesmen from farming the land for 3-4 years, and active hostilites continuing for so long that reconstruction of the village was not attempted until 1957, ten years after the disagreement started. Nor is active hostility an effective bar on intermarriage between chiefly families, as witnessed by the affinal ties between the Zarghamis and the Khan of the Kurdshuli, with whom the Basseri have always been at odds. However, such kinship between opposed chiefs is never activated by informal intervisiting, and cannot be used to cover an encroachment on the authority of the chief so related, as may kin ties between allied chiefs.

Contacts between different tribes are thus mediated through their respective chiefs, and thereby involve the whole tribe as a political corporation. Except inside the Khamseh confederacy, such contacts are few and pregnant with opposition and hostility — a condition which assures the persistence of the tribes as discrete social groups.

The importance of such inter-tribal relations has recently been on the decline, while the relation between the tribe and the sedentary authorities has become increasingly important. The significance of this relation to the position of the chief has been discussed; a more detailed description of its contemporary form would require an analysis of the sedentary political system far beyond the scope of this study. Only some major features of the situation can be indicated.

As noted, the Basseri tribe was put under direct Army administration two years ago. This means that whereas till then, all political relations with sedentary society had been on the corporate level, mediated by the chief, today the tribesmen can appeal to and deal directly with members of the Army hierarchy, culminating in the Colonel responsible for the Basseri and Kurdshuli tribes, who is accessible to any tribesman who desires to see him. Though there is some feeling that such individual dealings with the Colonel imply disloyalty to the deposed chief, they are increasingly frequent and accepted by all as inevitable in the circumstances. The contemporary dilemma of the tribesmen was perhaps most clearly revealed to me in a Mother-Goose-like ditty which the little girls sing, among many others, at festive gatherings: "Zarghami, don't beat me / don't beat me / it is not my fault / I am subject to the Army / and have no escape!"[1]

The fact of Army administration, however, does continue to insulate the tribesmen from direct contact with civil sedentary authorities. The Colonel, like the chief before him, mediates in the solution of conflicts when tribesmen are called before civil courts.

In most cases the chief also continues to mediate relations with the sedentary authorities, since appeals are constantly made to him by the tribesmen, and he himself is actively interested in their welfare. But his position is complicated, not only by his formal deposition, but also by the very complex and fluid political situation in which he must act. Numerous power structures are at least marginally interested in tribal affairs, and there is no effective division of their fields of authority. In addition to overlapping between different special governmental departments, there is also rivalry between the provincial authorities in Shiraz, and the even larger number of central national institutions in Teheran. The chief must deal with all of them, without offending any: with the local commanding General and the Headquarters in Teheran; with representatives in Parliament and with the secretariat for tribal affairs at the Shah's court; with the Provincial

---

[1] Zarghami nazan, nazan / taskhir nadaram / mashmul-e-chardowlatam / kafil nadaram.

Governor, the legal courts, and so on down to local pest control teams and the school-teacher in the one tribal school among the Basseri, who regularly abandons his post and runs away.

The chief can only hope to do this when he is a member of the local *élite* in Shiraz, and to some extent also of the strongly Teheran-oriented national *élite*. Only through such participation can he establish the net of informal contacts which are probably decisive to the opportune mobilization of the different administrative organs and the exercise of any significant influence. This means that he must keep a house in Shiraz and spend more and more time there, and must also travel on frequent visits to Teheran. The more frequent absence and consequent progressive alienation of the chief from his tribe is thus not only the result of his formal deposition and replacement by Army rule; it results from clear trends in the political constitution and administrative development of Iran, and produces a situation of real and fundamental crisis for the tribal systems of organization.

The external political relations of the tribe, never conspicuous for their structural simplicity, thus appear to be becoming increasingly multiplex. Their one consistent aspect is their corporate nature: that they are for all practical purposes all mediated by the central chief or his contemporary *alter,* the Colonel, on behalf of the tribe as a whole. But the tribe has other external relations than political ones — of fundamental importance to its whole pattern of subsistence is an intimate and continuous economic relationship with a sedentary market. It is striking that in this field corporate relations are entirely absent, and the tribal framework of organization is never mobilized, not even in the settlement of conflicts arising from economic exchanges in the market. Thus while, e.g., crop damage caused by a nomad's flock may lead to conflict involving civil and tribal authorities in opposition, the same nomad in a disagreement over a debt relationship with a villager cannot mobilize the support of his tribe. Economic relations remain separate and individual; their relevance to the organization and position of the tribe as a whole derives from their number and importance, providing an enmeshing effect whereby the tribe is related to the sedentary communities along its migration route by a great number of individual dyadic ties between its members and persons in the sedentary society.

The economic transactions of the nomads with this sedentary market take two forms: cash sales and purchases in the bazars of the larger towns, mainly Jahrom and Marvdasht, and credit relations with personal trading partners in the small villages.

Direct bazar sales and purchases represent only a small fraction of the turnover of a nomad household, but have a special importance because of the festive setting — for the nomads, such trips to town are great events. Camps are generally pitched some kilometres from town; and men, women and children dress in their best clothes and ride in, leaving only a few family members behind to look after the herds and property. The purpose of the bazar visit is to buy high-grade consumer goods, to be able to select from a wide variety the most appealing clothes, equipment, and luxury items. Some nomads bring ready money for these transactions; others bring livestock for sale to provide them with cash. On the outskirts of town, the nomads are therefore met by sedentary buyers of livestock, who make them offers and after much haggling generally close the deal. The Basseri are eager to sell to these agents, since they claim that the price they get on the livestock market place in the bazar is lower than what they can obtain on the outskirts of town, and also that the price falls steadily during the day, because the buyers know that the nomads are eager to obtain the cash, so that they can make their purchases and return to the tents before the afternoon. If this were the main factor affecting the price, however, it is difficult to explain why the buyers should go out to meet the nomads, rather than force the prices down by staying in the bazar.

The vast bulk of the Basseri's supplies of agricultural and industrial products is obtained in a different way, from trading partners usually referred to as "friends", in the smaller villages and from occasional travelling peddlers. Each nomad has stable relations with a number of such trading partners in villages scattered along the migration route of his section; the most important one, however, is the one in the winter area.

The trading relationship is first established on the villager's initiative — he comes out in the daytime among the nomad tents with donkeys loaded with a variety of goods, but returns to the village before nightfall, for fear of being robbed. The nomad who wishes to make an exchange invites the villager into his tent for tea, during which prices and forms of payment are discussed, and the social identity of the

98

nomad is established. Occasionally, and then only when there is a pre-established relationship, the nomad may solicit an exchange by bringing or sending pastoral products to the villager, specifying the goods he requires.

The villager usually gives his goods on credit, and in the winter and spring area continues to provide the nomad with what he needs during his whole period of residence. Then, a week or less before the nomad's departure, the villager comes to settle accounts. The value of the items that have been provided is added up, and paid for in products of corresponding current market value, mainly in clarified butter, cheese, hides, and rugs. Sheepshearing takes place later in the spring, so wool is exchanged mainly with villagers in the higher areas.

A debt is frequently left outstanding after this settlement; to be repaid after eight months, in the autumn, or next spring after a full year. These debts may run into considerable sums, not infrequently as much as 1,000 to 2,000 Tomans, i. e. £ 50-100. Some village partners charge an interest rate of 5-10 % p. a., but many waive their claim to any interest. This must mean that the villager's margin of profit on such transactions is high, since interest rates charged on debts between villagers are much higher, of the order of 30 %. One would otherwise have expected an even higher interest rate on the nomads' debts, since the risk on such loans is greater — on the other hand, perhaps these risks of default rise more steeply with greater interest charges, making exorbitant charges unprofitable.

Deferring of payment may be of great value to the nomad. If forced to make good a debt beyond the value of his current store of products such as milk products and wool, he must invade his productive capital in animals. While the market value of a ewe in 1958 was c. 80 T., the value of her total annual product was about the same (cf. p. 17) — in other words, his capital in herds gives a return of 100 % p. a., and may if retained enable him to make good considerable debts over a period of one year. Simultaneously large debts lead of course to a reduction of expenditures by the household, and consequently more rapid capital accumulation.

There is no written evidence of such debts; yet the nomads rarely appear to deny having received goods, and can be relied on to recognize their debts. The common form of escape is only by default and fleeing the territory in which their creditors live. But I was not able to discover any actual cases of this — presumably the villagers are shrewd enough not to give more credit than the value a nomad sets on his vested interests in a territory: his oulad pasture rights and community membership. Occasional losses to the village creditor must, however, occur through pauperization of their nomadic debtors, and their consequent sedentarization in other areas.

The various strands of the Basseri tribe's external relations may now be summarized. As noted, they fall very clearly into two classes: relations of a political nature, which are corporate, and economic marketing relations, in which each household acts as an independent unit. The former relations all involve the tribe as a whole, and are mediated by the chief: relations within the Khamseh confederacy, whereby the chief provides for the security of the tribe's estate; relations of hostility and competition with other tribes, which are expressed and controlled by the chief; and finally relations with the administrators of sedentary society, involving almost continuous negotiations and adjustments effected by the chief. In economic matters, on the other hand, each Basseri household stands entirely alone, and must deal with the agents of an impersonal, fluctuating world market. They adapt to this mainly by establishing dyadic ties with village traders, through which they perform economic exchanges and obtain the credit they require for effective budgeting. In spite of their vital importance to the economy of the tribe, the chief is not directly involved in any way as an under-writer for such credits. Indirectly, however, his presence is felt, since credit can be obtained from villagers only because of the great regularity and dependability of the movements of every nomad camp — a regularity which results only from the exercise of some of the chief's most vital functions.

*Camels and donkeys
in the caravan.*

*Hassan Ali Zarghami,
the chief of the Basseri,
beside a gazelle he has shot.
Behind him members
of the Darbar camp.*

*My host Ghulam, with his youngest daughter
and my assistant Ali Dad, in the tent.*

Chapter VIII

ECONOMIC PROCESSES

Other aspects of the economic organization of the Basseri also have important implications for the social organization of the tribe, and vice versa. Of particular importance are their organization into small economically independent households, and certain characteristic features of capital formation in a pastoral economy.

As we have seen, every Basseri obtains rights at birth in the pastures of his oulad. These rights are without restriction in the sense that there is no limit to the number of animals he may have on these pastures, so long as they are his own. The limiting factor on his income is thus the size of his privately owned flocks; any increase in them brings a rich return in increased profits harvested from the communally owned pastures. The immense interest in conserving and increasing the herds which is characteristic of the Basseri — as apparently of most pastoral people — thus has an economic justification.

For the Basseri to invest labour in anything else than the care of animals and in satisfying the immediate needs for comfort of the household members, would require forms of organization which are not found among them. Systematic division of labour within the tribe, or any investment of communal labour in the improvement of pastures or roads, requires for one thing a system for the distribution of foodstuffs, which is lacking, except where the chief uses his authority in an *ad hoc* manner to provide for such a system. Thus when he desires a large carpet to be made, the chief can call on labour — 10 to 12 women working full time for weeks or months — and provide them with food and facilities from his own large household; whereas in any other circumstances, only one or two women are able to work together, for a few hours each day, between cooking food and tending the animals.

But the chief uses this power to organize larger enterprises only to satisfy the particular needs of *his* household, and not for the benefit of the oulads or the tribe as a whole. Thus, for example, several large spring pasture areas in the south are never used, though the tribesmen say they would be excellent if there were only water available to the animals within practicable distance. All that would be required to open up these pastures would be the digging of a probably not very deep well; but the nomads have no way of organizing themselves for digging such a well as a communal project — who would tend their flocks while they were engaged in the work, and why should one particular camp do it, when the fruits of the labour would be reaped by dozens of other camps as well? Where sedentary communities establish themselves in such areas, each nomadic householder can obtain water as he needs it from them, sometimes in return for a small payment. If no such sources exist, the nomads are unable to utilize the pastures. They are organizationally equipped only to exploit a natural environment as it is, not to invest labour in modifying it for subsequent more efficient utilization.

All attention then becomes focused on the well-being of the herd; and great emphasis is placed on conserving it, on postponing every slaughter, so as to benefit from every day of growth and every season of increase. The result is a great deal of very careful living, whereby people of fair means continue to deny themselves all luxuries. The Basseri themselves are fully aware of this weakness of theirs, that borders on miserliness; it comes out in gossip about persons, and in the great value placed on hospitality as a mortal virtue. Extreme cases of miserliness are made the target of ridicule and condemnation in public — one of the wealthiest members of the tribe, who dresses poorly, rides a mule, never gives food to visitors, and works as shepherd of much of his own flocks, is known by the delightful nickname of D.D.T. Khan, with the implication that he is so miserly he eats his own lice.

Together with this attitude goes the great faith placed in the capacity of the animals to grow and multiply, the feeling that for the person with herding luck, one ewe will inevitably be transformed into large herds, given the necessary labour force of reliable shepherds. On

102

the other hand, there are large risk factors, of early frosts that may kill the lambs, drought that will sap the herd's health, and pests that will decimate it, leaving the once rich herd-owner a pauper.

A major part of the nomad's labour is thus invested in the care of the flocks, in increasing them and building them up. As soon as a man's herd passes a certain minimal threshold which is required for the subsistence of himself and his family, the rate of growth tends to increase; and during a succession of good years, a number of members of the tribe can become great herd-owners, with flocks of 200 to 800 head, and a few even more.

At this point, however, new factors set in, deriving from the nature of pastoral capital. It is a characteristic feature of wealth in herds that its net productivity rate for the owner declines as the size of the herds increases. No effective means have been developed among the Basseri to protect the rights of the big herd-owner — the less the flocks are under the owner's constant supervision, the more he will be cheated out of his profits while made to carry real or fictitious losses. Shepherds can — and the Basseri agree that given a chance, they inevitably will — be more careless of their master's flocks than they would of their own; they can sell livestock and claim the animals have been lost, pocketing the profits; if they have some animals of their own, they can provide them with the lambs of other ewes in case of accidents at lambing; they will consume part of the product of the herd, and sell part, claiming that production has been low, etc. etc. These possibilities are reflected in the terms of the contracts on which flocks are farmed out (cf. pp. 13-14), whereby for longer-term contracts, the original capital value is secured in one way or another, while the terms with regard to profit sharing are extremely liberal. Yet such contracts can not counteract the tendency towards an inverse correlation between rate of interest and size of capital.

What is more, the capital asset itself, the flock, is, as we have seen, subject to unpredictable fluctuations and severe losses from natural causes, averaging as much as 50 % in some disaster years; and these risks also increase with the less careful attention the flocks will receive from hired shepherds than from owners.

As a herd-owner's wealth grows, there are thus growing economic incentives for him to transfer a part of his capital to another form than wealth in herds — that is, to a form in which it gives a greater

103

marginal profit, and where the owner is more secure against capital losses. The latter condition is satisfied by various forms of stored wealth common among nomads, mainly carpets and female jewelry. Most families wish to have a certain amount of such goods to exhibit as symbols of status and wealth; but wealth in this form gives no economic returns. The only other imperishable form of wealth into which wealth in flocks can be converted in the traditional South Persian economy is *land* — a form which also gives a high rate of interest in the form of landlord's rents. The typical pattern for wealthy nomads is therefore to convert a fraction of their wealth in flocks into landed property. There is an active market in landed property in the area; such property can be freely subdivided and transferred to any buyer, and except in outlying areas, administrative supervision is good enough, so such transactions are simple economic matters, with reasonably effective police support for the rights of the legal title holder. Nomadic pastoralists are thus free to purchase land. Along their whole route of migration, they acquire plots of variable sizes and values, which they let out to villagers on the standard land tenancy contracts of the area.

Some of the features of land tenancy contracts, and the privileged position of landowners in sedentary Persian society, should be summarized, since they affect the volume of this flow of capital, and its sociological consequences.

Lambton (1953: 259) summarizes the situation for Persia as a whole as follows: ". . . . whereas the power and privileges of the landowning class have been relatively constant over a long period, its composition has undergone many changes. From time to time it has incorporated new elements into its ranks and lost others. Never, however, has a stable landed aristocracy, transmitting its estates in their entirety from generation to generation, emerged." The nomad entering the ranks of the petty landlords thus does not meet with any strong social barriers; by virtue of the simple fact of title to land he exercises full privileges as a member of the land-owning class. These are considerable.

Vis-à-vis the tenants, his title gives him the right freely to dispose of his land — the peasants have no traditional usufruct rights, and in fact no legal security of tenure. In most places, fields are arbitrarily allotted on annual tenancy contracts as the landlord sees fit; where there is a very definite pattern of rotation of crops, the contract period is usually extended to the termination of one full cycle, or a period of 2-3 years. In most areas there is over-population and competition between tenants for contracts; few men are provided with as much land as they are able, and wish, to cultivate. The terms of the contracts are thus throughout very advantageous to the land-owner. They vary a great deal locally, but generally give the land-owner 1/3-1/2 of unirrigated crops and 1/2-2/3 of irrigated crops. In the summer pasture areas, with more marginal agriculture, land values are low and the owner's share of the crop is reduced to 1/6 of the total crop.

The tenants are expected by these contracts to supply all labour, animals, and farm equipment; but the landlord often gives seed. Though all formal traces of a feudal pattern of organization have disappeared, a landlord still wields great powers over his tenants. They must submit to his detailed control and supervision in most fields of life, not only in those directly connected with their work. Where the property is of any size, or the landlord is an absentee owner, this control is generally exercised through the landlord's appointed agent (*katkhoda*).

In the wider society, too, the position of even a petty landowner is one of relative privilege. His title to land gives him entry into the local *élite* of his village and district, and in the case of wealthier landlords, also on a provincial or national level. In dealings with the local authorities, the man who owns land, however small the plot may be, is in an entirely different position from the ordinary villager.

A transfer of capital from flocks into land holdings is thus economi-cally advantageous to the wealthier herd-owner; it also offers striking social advantages within the framework of sedentary society. A number of Basseri choose to do this — frequently with no thoughts of future sedentarization. The land provides them with a secure store of wealth and a considerable annual income in the agricultural products needed in their normal pattern of consumption — it frees them from the necessity of purchasing these products and thus tends to increase the rate of growth of their herds. Unless disease strikes their herds severely, the process tends to become cumulative, with a steadily growing frac-tion of the nomad's wealth invested in land. The greater these interests in land are, the more the owner becomes motivated to supervise and control his property; and he thus finds himself drawn increasingly into the in many ways very comfortable and privileged status of sedentary landlord. Once a certain point in the development has been passed, disasters striking the herds serve merely to end his engagement in pastoral activities. A number of Basseri in every generation pass through this development, and end up as sedentary landlords in villages in or near the Basseri migration channel, frequently camping in tents in the gardens of their houses half the year, and with a continuing emotional interest in and identification with nomad life and ways.

One brief life history may serve to illustrate this process. The man in question was a member of the Labu Musa section, and is now 50-55 years old. When he was 15, he started with 20 sheep and one donkey. His herd grew steadily, because of his herding skill and luck (though his enemies whisper that he augmented the natural growth of his herd by theft — a common accusation against the too prosperous). Very soon he started setting aside the value of about 20 sheep p. a. as savings; he also traded in hides. After some years he bought a piece of land by Band Amir. During the period of enforced settlement under Reza Shah he built a house, but never lived in it, and continued to migrate by bribing the police, thereby conserving his pastoral wealth through a period of great difficulties for most nomads. In 1956 he bought a larger compact block of land further north, by selling his land in Band Amir and elsewhere as well as most of his animals. On his new property he has constructed a good house and lives as a settled landowner with two wives and several small children, in considerable comfort. The few hundred head of sheep that he still owns are farmed out with relatives among the Labu Musa on the usual contracts.

Growth in the wealth of a pastoral nomad may thus, in certain circumstances, have cumulative effects that result in the nomad's quitting his tribe and his pastoral pursuits, and becoming assimilated into sedentary society as a petty landowner. This happens with considerable frequency; but there are features of Basseri organization which prevent it from becoming the predominant pattern. The most important of these features is the normal cycle of family development, which serves as a brake on extreme capital accumulation in the hands of one person. As we have noted, sons receive their patrimony at the time of marriage, which means that the fragmentation of a man's

106

herd sets in around the middle, rather than the end, of his adult life. Its timing also has some correlation with the wealth of the man: the poor man postpones the expense of his son's marriage till the boy is 30 or even 35 years old; a wealthier man is subject to strong pressures, both from public opinion and from his son, to arrange for the boy's marriage shortly after he is 20 years old. The greater the labour supply a man controls, in the form of sons who can assist him as shepherd boys, and the greater his success at accumulating wealth, the shorter is the period in which his herd grows, before it starts being subdivided and passing on to other hands. A man thus has not much more than twenty years, in a normally fertile marriage, within which the whole sedentarization process must be completed: from the time he starts a marriage, with his initial flock, till his sons start claiming their shares of the estate. Only childless men, or men with only daughters, can expect a cumulative growth of their herds throughout their life — but they, on the other hand, do not control the additional male labour required for rapid expansion.

An additional factor is the practice of polygyny. Wealthy herd owners frequently enter plural marriages, since they are in a position to secure and support an additional wife, and need additional female labour, as well as desiring the sexual services of a younger woman. Such marriages extend the period of a man's fecundity in a way that usually saps his wealth further: not only must he continue to support unproductive children over a long period; the system of anticipatory inheritance is such that marrying sons will tend to receive "too large" shares of the estate. This will happen, since the fraction which a son receives at marriage is computed on the basis of the number of living, unmarried sons at that moment. Additional male issue, born at a later date, have full rights on their father's estate without by their presence having reduced the share allotted to those of their brothers who were already married when the later births took place.

I have no reliable data on the numerical frequency of sedentarization as a result of capital accumulation, as compared to the frequency of rapid fragmentation and redistribution of such wealth, and a continuation of a pastoral subsistence for the persons involved. Settled, landowning Basseri are found scattered over a very large area; but it is safe to say that the latter pattern, of fragmentation and redistribution, is the one of greater importance to Basseri social organization — it is the process which takes place within Basseri nomadic society, and which serves as a regular mechanism to maintain its present form.

Whereas the flocks tend to prosper and grow due to the nomad's work in herding and tending them, accidents, pests and mismanagement may also have the obverse effect of reducing the herds through time; or the needs of the pastoralist may be too great, and lead him to over-tax his herd, and result in a decline in the herder's wealth, rather than an accumulation. As we have seen, all such economic risks are carried in their entirety by the separate, individual households. Each Basseri household depends for its subsistence on its privately owned flocks, except for the small number of hired herdsmen who support themselves by selling their labour; so without their animals, most households would be debarred from continuing a nomadic existence as members of the tribe. Serious loss of wealth in a household thus has the result that the household is sloughed off from the tribe; or, to put it the other way around, the persistence of the present form of Basseri organization depends on a continual process of sloughing-off of members who fail to retain the productive capital in herds which is required for an independent pastoral existence. The process of sloughing-off, or sedentarization by impoverishment, depends precisely on the non-corporate nature of all market relations, described in the previous chapter.

The nomads are familiar with this process, in its various steps; it has happened and happens continually about them in their own tribe and section; and it is felt as a threatening and live possibility in a number of households of the lower economic range. Its stages are gradual and, though they may be fought against tooth and nail, have an impersonal and overwhelming feeling of inevitability about them.

The first stage is that of carrying large debts to a trading partner over from one year to the next. Chances are that, in spite of moderate herding luck, only a part of the debt can be paid off next year, in addition to the financing of the family's needs during that year. To meet such debts, and the running demands of his household, the herder is forced to invade his productive capital, slaughtering female lambs and selling livestock. Once this downward spiral starts, it tends to accelerate in spite of all efforts to cut down on consumption — the disparity between the minimal rate of consumption and the productivity of the declining capital grows geometrically. The figure of 60 adult sheep and goats seems at the time of my field-work to have been regarded as the threshold below which a downward movement was inevitable for a normal household.[1] If large flocks on tenancy terms are not available (and crises of this kind are generally set off by natural events which strike all, and reduce the already small number of herds available on such contracts), then such households must seek other temporary sources to augment their income, all of them connected with sedentary communities.

There are a number of temporary and seasonal occupations of this kind open to the nomad: in harvesting, or guarding winter crops and stores, or as shepherd for a village flock, or by using donkeys in local transport or trading. Common to all these are the need for the nomad to establish an enduring association with one particular village or another, and to be stationary during the period of his work for that village. While this opens the way for the development of more intimate bonds with villagers, both personal and economic, it also usually accelerates the rate of reduction of the nomad's remaining herd by interfering with the normal migratory cycle. The result thus tends to be further loss of animals, loss of contact with the nomad's own tent group, increased dependence on sources of income within a village, and eventual integration into the sedentary community in the status of propertyless villager.

That the process of sedentarization, of "passing" from nomadic to settled society, should have these two basic forms might in fact have been deduced from first principles by comparing the status systems of the tribe and the South Persian villages. The situation might be diagrammatically expressed as in figure 7. In the village, there is an extreme gulf between the privileged and wealthy landowner and the subject and practically propertyless peasantry. In the tribe, common tribesmen are subject to their chief, but retain considerable rights and freedoms, and they have enough privately owned capital to permit them to be self-employed. In the wider Persian status system, tribesmen thus occupy a position intermediate between landowner and peasants; and in the South Persian tenancy villages there is no status

---

[1] Several tents of the camp with which I spent most of my time had fallen below this point; and I am told that two of them have now, 1½ years later, become sedentary.

109

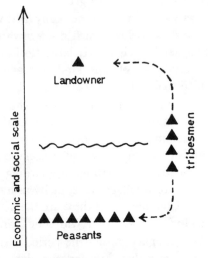

Fig. 7. *Routes of sedentarization.*

position on a corresponding level. For the bulk of the tribesmen, assimilation into village society in either of its major statuses is not feasible, even if it were desired: to be a landowner, they would require vastly larger capital than they in fact control, accompanied by an unrealistic increase in status, while to become a tenant would imply a shattering loss of status. Only the top and the bottom of the nomadic economic spectrum are at all comparable to the statuses found in the village community; and only for them can one see any motives that might encourage sedentarization: those near the top can thereby secure their capital and have their higher status confirmed; those near the bottom are already reduced to a position of poverty and submission like the tenant, and are driven to the village to secure work and their own survival.

Within the framework of Basseri social organization, economic processes are thus at work. The pattern of organization requires each adult man to have a certain minimum of wealth; and this wealth must be in the form of live herds of sheep and goats — a form continually dependent on replacement, and subject to unpredictable fluctuations of growth and loss. Radical departures from the middle range of wealth, except for the person of the chief, cannot be accommodated within the organization; and they must either be com-

110

pensated for and thus corrected, or the deviant household must be eliminated from the tribe.

Various mechanisms have been described which set in and compensate for fluctuations. In cases of loss of wealth, these are: reduced consumption, debts at interest rates appreciably lower than the rate of production of pastoral capital, postponement of the normal process of subdivision and multiplication of households by the marriage of sons, and occasional shepherding of the animals of others on advantageous terms. In cases of excessive accumulation of wealth, they are: increased consumption, decline in the rate of productivity of the capital, early subdivision of the household, and its division into an increased number of new units receiving disproportionate shares of the original estate. Where these mechanisms fail, as they frequently do, to compensate fully for growth or loss of herds, sedentarization takes place. In cases of excessive accumulation of wealth, the sedentarization process has a form where it remains subject to compensating mechanisms throughout, and socially has the appearance of a kind of reluctant upward mobility. In cases of impoverishment, its sets in after the compensatory mechanisms have failed, and is associated with a rapid economic collapse. As one would expect from these characteristics, all numerical evidence suggests that sedentarization by impoverishment is the numerically predominant form.

Chapter IX

DEMOGRAPHIC PROCESSES

The previous chapters have sought to reveal the different processes which influence and determine Basseri social forms. Some of these processes are internal to the tribe, such as those governing the formation of camp groups; others have to do with the relations of the tribe to its environment, both physical and social. For the social organization to remain even moderately stable, these processes must produce an approximate balance. With respect to the relations between the tribe and its environment, this balance may be analysed in terms of several systems into which the tribe enters; and I have tried to show the place of the Basseri, in this respect, within the systems of the ecology, economy, and politics of South Persia. The Basseri maintain a short-term *ecologic* balance with the environment by migrations and winter dispersal, whereby the intensity of utilization of pastures is adjusted to the carrying capacity of the different pastures at the different seasons, while the long-term balance between flocks and pastures is beyond the control of the tribesmen, and depends mainly on natural growth rates on the one hand, and disease and taxation on the other. The Basseri also maintain an approximate *economic* and *political* balance with their external social environment, mediated through market exchanges, and the institution of centralized chieftaincy.

One further type of relation with the environment remains to be analysed. For the present form of organization to persist, the Basseri tribe must also have a moderately stable population — i. e. it must be in *demographic* balance. Since the tribe is only a partial isolate within the larger population of the area, the factors involved in this balance are both biological and social: on the one hand natural fecundity and social accretion, on the other hand birth-control, death-rate, and mobility both in the forms of emigration and sedentarization.

Any systematic analysis of these factors requires demographic data of a type and reliability that does not as yet exist for the tribes. The numerical data which it was possible for me to collect first-hand on these topics are naturally very limited and incomplete, and can serve only to suggest some very general trends. However, their implications for the analysis of the organization of the tribe are so great that I feel they require some discussion.

The general level of nutrition and hygiene among the Basseri appears quite high. The population is generally healthy and robust, with an associated high fertility rate. With marriage taking place some time between the ages of 16-20 years, women have a long child-bearing period, and frequently a woman gives birth to her last child well after her eldest daugther gives birth to her first.

Reliable figures on the fertility rate of the tribe could only be derived from material collected over a long period, since the statements of informants on such a topic are hardly reliable. A certain index of this rate, however, is given by ordinary census counts. In a tent camp containing 32 living married couples, the average number of children at the time of my census was 4.25 per couple. In this sample are a scatter of couples from recently married to spouses who have passed their reproductive period. No couple in this camp was infertile, and only few cases of infertility were met with elsewhere in the tribe. Since few people know their own age, or the date of their marriage, it is impossible to break down this population into meaningful age categories. None the less, the figure 4.25 gives an indication of a high reproductive rate in the population.

Of the controls on natural growth, birth control is limited to herbal medicines of doubtful efficacy, and these are used mainly by women who have already produced a number of children, since plentiful issue are invariably desired by both parents. In view of the generally healthier conditions in the tent camps than in villages, one would expect infant and child mortality to be appreciably lower than in the villages of the area, though doubtless high by European standards. Even during migration, infants are not exposed to particular rigours, e. g. of heat or cold, that could cause exceptional deaths.

114

Periodic plagues and epidemics, on the other hand, such as till recently ravaged the area, have been an important control on population growth in South Persia. Older informants remember disasters, when people died so quickly and in such numbers that they were left, unburied, along the roadside. Famines, on the other hand, never seem to have been a major direct threat, though periods of want may have had their effect in reducing the natural resistance of the tribesmen to disease.

All the evidence indicates that the balance between the factors of natural fecundity, and the natural controls of death-rate and birth control gives a high net rate of natural growth within the tribe. This net rate is indicated by the size of adult sibling groups. Since in each generation there is a dispersal of kin, such data are difficult to collect and check. But in the Darbar section, in which I did most work, I found the representatives of 13 sibling groups in the general age range 20-50, the sizes of which I could check by questioning one or both of the surviving parents, as well as the members themselves. In these 13 sibling groups, I found the staggering figure of an average of 7.2 live members per sibling group.

The Basseri themselves are very well aware of this high rate of increase, and it is discussed with great pride. Thus 600 bilateral descendants were claimed for Haji Mohammed Khan, the father's father of the present chief, while Kal Ali Baz of Il-e-Khas bragged of having fathered 24 children from two wives, and the headman of Oulad-e-Qazem, Kolumbei proudly reported that his deceased father, Haji Sultan Ali, has a total of 20 sons and sons' sons alive today.

There is no reason to think that this rate of increase is recent, or unique for the generation born 20-50 years ago. The figures on present fertility seem consistent with those of the previous generation; and in the period 1908-38 in which that generation was born, none of the effects of modern medicine could yet have been felt, even indirectly, in the nomad camps of Fars. One is thus forced to assume that a consistently high rate of growth has been a characteristic of the tribal population in previous times as well as today. The evidence from the living generations in the Basseri camps today — 4.25 children per tent, and 7.2 persons per adult sibling group — suggests a net growth factor of at least 3 per generation, i. e. a trebling of the nomad population every 30-40 years. This general

115

picture is, furthermore, not unique for the Basseri; superficial acquaintance with neighboring Arab and Qashqai suggest comparable natural growth rates.

Since nomadic tribes of a basic economy and organization similar to the Basseri are of great antiquity in the area, one may be justified in assuming that the total tribal population is and has been in approximate demographic balance, i. e. that there are processes which drain off at least a major fraction of this natural increase in every generation. These processes are emigration, and sedentarization.

Repeatedly in the past, groups have defected from the tribe and the area, to move either northward to the Isfahan area and beyond, or eastward into Kerman. During the rule of Agha Jan Beg (cf. p. 73) a number of such defections took place. For example, according to the traditions of the Il-e-Khas, a total of 300 tents left as a group to join in the new tribe then being formed by Zel-e-Sultan, a son of Nasr-ud-Din Shah, in Isfahan, while about 30 tents of Il-e-Khas went east to Kerman, and a remnant of 8-10 houses only of that section remained behind as settlers near Band Amir, where their descendants live today. But reverse movements also take place, of tribal splinters *from* other places moving *to* the Basseri area; so it is doubtful whether the net effect of such movements serves to relieve or increase the population pressure among the Basseri and allied tribes.

The other process effecting a flow of population from the Basseri, and from nomadic life in general, is sedentarization. We have seen the economic processes which produce such a flow; and detailed inquiries into the families of members even of rapidly growing sections show that this drain on population growth is both considerable, and of long standing. The accompanying genealogy of male members of a patriline in one such growing section illustrates the role of seden-

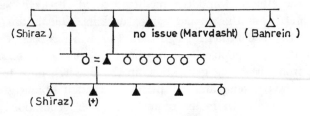

Fig. 8. Cases of sedentarization in one family history.

The baby of the tent in his hammock.
Note the pile of household goods
which forms a low partition
towards the back of the tent.

Girls preparing balls of cheese (kashk)
for drying.

tarization in the history of a fairly representative family. Persons marked in black have remained in the tribe, while those in white have become settled. In the present adult generation, the person marked with (+) had in 1958 bought roof timbers and was considering settling in Marvdasht.

Another form of sedentarization is in large groups, preferably in compact settlements, such as that of several sections of the Ali Mirzai part of the tribe in villages in their traditional summer pastures in Chardonge. Most of the current sections of the Basseri also have recognized collateral settled branches in some localities. Thus, e. g. the Farhadi have the following subdivisions:

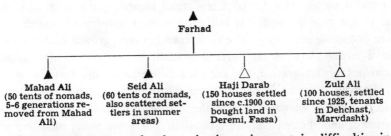

Mahad Ali	Seid Ali	Haji Darab	Zulf Ali
(50 tents of nomads, 5-6 generations removed from Mahad Ali)	(60 tents of nomads, also scattered settlers in summer areas)	(150 houses settled since c.1900 on bought land in Deremi, Fassa)	(100 houses, settled since 1925, tenants in Dehchast, Marvdasht)

This high frequency of sedentarization raises certain difficulties in the interpretation of the demographic data. It suggests a mechanism whereby a net population increase may be drained off; it also, if it has any appreciable frequency, may give a bias to the very data on which the rate of this increase is estimated. The analysis of sedentarization (pp. 105-11) uncoved certain selective factors in the recruitment of settlers, one of which is the absence of male issue. I also tried to show in the analysis of the organization of the camp the particular importance of numerous siblings and children for securing a person's position in nomad society. There is thus reason to believe that childless couples, couples with only daughters, and persons belonging to small sibling groups show a higher frequency of sedentarization than do highly fertile members of larger sibling groups. The former thus tend to be removed from the nomad population, and statistical data on fertility collected on a sample of adults within the nomad camps will give exaggerated averages of the size of sibling groups. The actual effect of this selective factor is difficult to evaluate — that it should be a major factor in creating the impression of a high fertility and natural growth rate is, however, out of the question.

117

The considerable growth of the Basseri tribe over the last generations doubtless reflects an internal growth of the population, as well as the process of accretion whereby foreign nomad groups become attached to dynamic and effective chiefs. But even from those sections which have grown most rapidly there has been a constant flow of settlers. It is clear that the net growth rate of the population must be so high that a group may grow quickly by natural increase even while giving off a major fraction of the excess growth of population through individual and collective sedentarization. Furthermore, whereas the tribe as a whole is growing, some of its component sections are experiencing a decline. The fertility rate within these sections, as revealed by my censuses of a few small camps, seems to be as high as in the growing sections; but a far greater number of households are becoming sedentary. The difference between growth and decline in a section depends on differences in their rates of sedentarization and possibly emigration, and not on a difference in their fertility rates.

In evaluating the demographic effects of sedentarization, the opposite movement of persons *from* the village *to* the tribe must be considered, and the net balance estimated. There are today members of the tribe who were born of tenant parents in villages, and have become nomads through choice, usually after a period of service as shepherds for others; and there is a greater number of nomads who trace descent from sedentary ancestors two, three or more generations removed, as do even some whole oulads (e. g. Ali Marduni of Abduli) and sections (Jouchin, Salvestuni). The rates of movements into and out of the villages are according to the Basseri sensitive to economic and political conditions: in times of peace and strong administration, the flow towards the villages increases, while in times of economic stress and chaos, such as Persia has experienced at regular intervals throughout her history till today, villagers and even whole sedentary communities may assume nomadic life. The over-all balance, however, as judged from my own material and by Basseri, is overwhelmingly in the direction of sedentarization.

On the assumption that similar processes are at work in the other nomadic tribes of the Fars area, some puzzling features of the local history become understandable. A number of Ali Mirzai sections of the Basseri have completely disappeared within the memory of old people, without leaving any traces suggesting assimilation into the

118

rapidly growing Weisi sections. On a larger scale, recent South Persian history can report on large tribes and confederacies, such as, e. g. the Lak Lurs of Fars on which Karim Khan Zand based his power in the late 18th century (Sykes 1921 II: 277) — tribes which today have left no visible trace in the local nomad population. I found that tribal maps and lists of tribal names, collected and compiled at the time of the First World War, caused great mirth when I showed them to the Basseri, since, as they said, contemporary tribes and tribes long since defunct were there listed side by side. All this becomes understandable if it is possible that the rate of sedentarization, in certain circumstances, can rise well above a tribal group's fertility rate, leading to that group's complete elimination from the nomadic scene. This indeed is what happened within the Khamseh confederacy to the Ainalu in the 1870-80's, and the Baharlu around 1900[1].

There is, however, also the other side of the picture to consider: the capacity of sedentary society in Fars to assimilate settlers. If the estimated fertility rate of the Basseri is at all realistic and representative of the nomadic population of Fars, the populations involved in sedentarization are of no mean magnitude. The nomad population of Fars has been estimated variously at different times at roughly 100,000 (Curzon 1892, II: 112-14), 250,000 (Sykes 1921, II: 477-80), and 400,000 (Demorgny 1913: 92-129). Of these, Sykes' figures on the Khamseh correspond closely to estimates for that period which I was given by Ghavam; his estimate of a total of 250,000 is probably the best.

The sedentary population of Fars province has since 1945 experienced an explosive growth due to large-scale public health measures, largely under U. N. auspices, and is claimed now to be about 2 million; Field's estimate (1939: 211) of 500,000 in 1918 is perhaps conservative, but there is every reason to believe that it has until recently been less than 1 million.

The nomadic population of Fars has thus until the last decade or two constituted at least 1/4 of the population of the province; a growth and sedentarization rate like that implied in the data presented above then seems hardly credible, since it would mean that half the sedentary population in every generation was recruited from the

[1] These date estimates by Basseri informants are confirmed from documentary sources by Lambton 1953: 159.

tribes, i. e. that the sedentary population of Fars was formerly unable to reproduce itself, and showed a very large population deficit. I have found no data on the demographic structure of villages in Fars; but there are strong suggestions that the fertility rate is low, infant mortality high, and emigration, both northward and abroad, common. Furthermore, there are also the dramatic population controls of epidemics and famine to consider. The nomads are less subject to contagion, since they live dispersed and tend to flee from contagion into the uninhabited hills and mountains when an epidemic strikes; and they are practically free from the threat of famine, with their large store of food in the form of herds. The villagers, on the other hand, are normally undernourished; they are packed together in unhygienic villages, often with a very poor and polluted water supply, and are therefore much more subject to contagion and to disease. Furthermore, all of Fars lies in the zone of Persia subject to locust invasions and consequent crop disasters and famines.

The effects of these conditions on the local sedentary population are revealed by occasional references in the literature. At times, travellers in Fars have found whole areas decimated and even depopulated as a result of plagues, typhus, and other epidemics (e. g. Rich 1836 II, who himself died as a victim of such an epidemic in Shiraz; Abbott 1857: 158, 180; Monteith 1857: 118; Sykes 1921, II: 515). For Persia as a whole, the population was estimated at 10 million in 1850, but in 1873, after two desolating visitations of cholera and famine, at 6 million (Curzon 1892; II: 492). As well as striking the nomad population and reducing their population excess, such disasters have primarily served to keep down the reproductive rate of the villages and towns, and to clear whole areas for sedentarization by nomads. The patchwork ethnic composition of the settled districts in Fars can be explained as one result of such a series of accidental exterminations and resettlements.

The demographic data needed to evaluate these trends properly are lacking; the few figures included in this discussion can only serve to suggest the possible order of magnitude of the population imbalances and movements in Fars. But all the data fit the general schema which I have outlined: that considerable nomad populations have consistently produced a large population excess in every generation, which through sedentarization has been assimilated into villages, and there has served to close a major gap between a low fertility rate and a high death rate in the sedentary population. The present form of nomad organization cannot persist unless this population excess is drawn off somehow — an accumulation of population would lead to overtaxing of pastures and flocks, economic collapse, and new organizational needs — a complex of phenomena that will be explored further in the next chapter. A comprehensive analysis of Basseri social organization can thus not be made without reference also to these interrelations between the nomadic and settled populations.

Chapter X

THE FORMS OF NOMADIC ORGANIZATION
IN SOUTH PERSIA

It should now be possible to draw together some of the major features of the preceding description and analysis. In the presentation so far, I have focused specifically on the Basseri tribe of the Khamseh confederacy, among whom my participant observation was done. But in the analysis of this material I have tried to show how the forms of Basseri organization reflect various features of their cultural premises and environment. In other words, I have tried to discover the fundamental processes whereby Basseri forms of organization are produced and maintained. Since the relevant features of the environment, and most of the cultural premises current among the Basseri, seem to have a wide distribution in Fars and adjoining areas, the processes which affect nomadic life elsewhere in South Persia should be essentially similar to those observed among the Basseri. The model of Basseri organization which I shall summarize should therefore also be useful in elucidating the organizational forms of neighboring tribes, and in explaining variations in form in terms of limited variations in the relevant factors of environment and culture.

Firstly, the various aspects of the ecologic and economic adaptation of the Basseri must be drawn together and their interrelations explored, to determine whether the activities and processes described are sufficient to maintain a stable population through time. The Basseri cultural premises which are relevant to this are essentially summed up in the principle of individual private ownership of animals. While pastures are shared within oulads and may be reallotted between them, the productive capital in animals which is necessary for a nomadic

123

subsistence is private property, and nomadic households can only survive when their members own a sufficient amount of such property.

The stability of a pastoral population depends on the maintenance of a balance between pastures, animal population, and human population. The pastures available by their techniques of herding set a maximal limit to the total animal population that an area will support; while the patterns of nomadic production and consumption define a minimal limit to the size of herd that will support a human household.

In this double set of balances is summarized the special difficulty in establishing a population balance in a pastoral economy: the human population must be sensitive to imbalances between flocks and pastures. Among agricultural, or hunting and collecting people, a crude Malthusian type of population control is sufficient. With a growing population, starvation and death-rate rise, until a balance is reached around which the population stabilizes. Where pastoral nomadism is the predominant or exclusive subsistence pattern, the nomad population, if subjected to such a form of population control, would *not* establish a population balance, but would find its whole basis for subsistence removed. Quite simply, this is because the productive capital on which their subsistence is based is not simply land, it is animals — in other words *food*. A pastoral economy can only be maintained so long as there are no pressures on its practitioners to invade this large store of food. Once it has been consumed, the population can no longer pursue a pastoral subsistence. A pastoral population can therefore only reach a stable level if other effective population controls intervene *before* those of starvation and death-rate.

A first requirement in such an adaptation is the presence of the patterns of private ownership of herds, and individual economic responsibility for each household. By these patterns, the population becomes fragmented with respect to economic activities, and economic factors can strike differentially, eliminating some members of the population without affecting other members of the same population. This would be impossible if the corporate organization with respect to political life, and pasture rights, were also made relevant to economic responsibility and survival.

With this basic adaptation, the various processes described in previous chapters suffice to maintain a balance between pastures, herds, and people — they combine to produce a self-regulating "feed-back"

124

system. To demonstrate this, the mechanisms of short-term and long-term balance are most readily discussed separately.

A short-term balance between pastures and herds is maintained by the pattern of migration, whereby the herds are dispersed or concentrated according to the productivity of the pastures, and utilize widely separated pasture areas at their different periods of productivity. I have shown in greater detail elsewhere (Barth 1960) the way in which the different tribes of Fars, through an organization in terms of regular migration routes and schedules, together utilize the pastures of Fars approximately to their total carrying capacity through the year.

The short-term balance between herds and human population is maintained individually by the different households. If they approach the minimal limit to the required size of herd, they reduce their level of consumption, obtain credit from villagers, and postpone the normal process of subdivision, thereby permitting their flocks to increase to a point where normal patterns may be resumed.

The effects of these balances between private herds and households, however, is to produce a correlation between the growth of the total herds of a tribe and the growth of its population. We have seen that the Basseri fertility rate is high; here we see, furthermore, that it is *not* sensitive to a growing pressure of larger herds on the available pastures. In other words, a long-term balance between pastures, herds and people is *not* maintained by changes in the human fertility rate.

The discussion of demographics demonstrated that the effective control on population growth is not starvation and thereby reduced fertility and increased death-rate, but, as one would expect from the considerations advanced here, other controls, primarily that of sedentarization. A long-term balance between pastures, herds and people and a consequent stable pastoral population can only be maintained if the rate of *sedentarization* is sensitive to the population pressure of *animals* on the pastures.

This condition does in fact obtain. Of the two forms of sedentarization described, each shows a correlation with different phases of growth in the total size of herds. With growing herds, the frequency of sedentarization by upward mobility — the accumulation of wealth and its transfer to landed property — increases. In payment for such land, animals are drawn off from the Basseri herds and transferred to sedentary buyers, and both the human and animal population of the

125

tribe are thus reduced. As for sedentarization through impoverishment, this strikes in a later phase of growth. While the nomadic human population is not directly subject to Malthusian controls, the animal population is. Overpopulation results in poor health and reduced fertility among the flocks. And most important, this poor health and the increased density makes the animal population increasingly susceptible to epidemic animal diseases. Such diseases sweep the area and reduce the animal population; what is more, they strike randomly and differentially in the privately owned herds of the pastoralists, reducing some of them below the minimum required for a pastoral subsistence, while hardly touching others. Those struck in that way are forced by impoverishment to become sedentary, while those whose flocks remain above the minimum are unaffected. Because of the pattern of economic organization, animal epidemics thus serve as a control not only on the size of the animal population, but also on the human nomad population of the area[1].

The manner in which the growth of the nomad population is checked by controls different from the ultimate controls of starvation and death rate should thus be clear. Because of the nomads' different techniques for maintaining short-term balance between pastures, herds, and households, the size of the animal population reflects the size of the human population. But animal population growth beyond a certain point tends to be checked by controls, which strike in such a way as to increase the rate of sedentarization, and thus reduce also the human population. It is an essential prerequisite for a stable pastoral population that such controls are effective, and that they precede the biological controls on human populations of reduced fertility and increased death-rate.

Such an essentially stable nomadic population offers the basis for the development of the social forms exhibited by the Basseri. On this same foundation, varying forms of organization may be developed. Perhaps most striking in South Persia is the variation in political forms. While the Basseri have essentially a single, autocratic chief, ruling a homogeneous population of subjects, the Qashqai to the west have a much more complex hierarchy of leaders, consisting of chiefs,

---

[1] Under different ecologic circumstances, particularly where sedentarization is impossible, other patterns, such as aggressive raiding and warfare, can effect a similar control on a nomad population.

126

headmen, and commoners; while in the areas to the East of the Basseri, including some of the Arab tribes of the Khamseh and extending on towards Kerman, are nomad tribes without any strong centralized chiefship at all. It is an interesting problem to explore the factors which may be responsible for such differences, on the background of the preceding analysis of the processes which affect Basseri organizational forms.

The areas that concern us differ somewhat in the scope they offer for a pastoral economy; they may be ranged on an ecologic east-west gradient. The areas in the west have higher mountain chains and greater precipitation; pastures are rich and the distances between good winter and summer pastures small. Passing eastward the country becomes increasingly drier, and the area and quality, particularly of the summer pastures, decrease, terminating in the Lut desert.

On this ecologic background, the political forms found among the Qashqai and in Kerman may be analysed with reference to the model which has been presented of Basseri organization. In my analysis of the Basseri I tried to show how the position and authority of the chief are related to the political constitution of the Basseri camps. In such a camp, the component tents are economically unconnected with each other, each man owns sufficient herds and has grazing rights by virtue of his oulad membership. Camp communities are maintained through the daily repeated process of reaching unanimity by mutual persuasion; and consequently no strong leaders, or crystallized factions, emerge within them. The chief, with some external sources of authority, is able to dominate such camps in autocratic fashion; in return for economic advantages for himself, and politico-military support, he contributes to the welfare of the tribe by mediating their relations with the sedentary society, and defends each man's rights to pastures through regulating the migrations.

The homogeneity of the camp, on which its political constitution is based, is a result of the characteristic patterns of sedentarization. Since wealth in land is more secure than wealth in herds, few men have very large herds, but tend to transfer their excess wealth to land and become sedentary. Chiefs are also aware of the threat to their authority which the really big herd owners represent; they may exert pressure to remove them, or the big herd owners fear that the chief on some pretext will seize their flocks, and are thereby induced to make

127

the change. The absence of such large herds, on the other hand, forces the impoverished nomad also to become sedentary, since few positions as servants and shepherds can be found.

If the possibility to transfer capital from animals to title in land is blocked, one may predict certain definite changes in this organization. Big herd owners would retain their wealth in herds and not be removed from the camp community; to tend and guard their flocks they would need to employ additional labour, and a fraction of the impoverished nomads would thus also be able to remain in camp, tied to wealthy employers. In other words, very considerable differences in status and power would develop in the camp, with clear consequences for the decision-making process within that group. It is reasonable to assume that patterns of effective leadership, and the crystallization of factions and a wider ramifying hierarchy of leaders would result. A central chief confronted with this situation would need to develop certain coercive organs to support his authority.

From what I have been able to learn about the Qashqai[1], this is roughly the organizational pattern which they exhibit. The Qashqai, of course, are a unit of the structural order of the whole Khamseh; but within the component tribes of the Qashqai, of sizes comparable to the Basseri, there appear to be a considerably greater internal hierarchization of political offices, and greater difference in wealth, than are found among the Basseri. The Amaleh of the Qashqai, corresponding to the Basseri Darbar, also seems to have much more the character of a specialized coercive institution and bodyguard, paralleling the forms found among other nomad groups further north (Barth 1953: 52).

Though I have no clear evidence on the patterns of sedentarization within the tribe, their environment is such as to suggest the absence, until recently, of sedentarization by upward mobility. This follows in part from the ecologic factors noted above. With the richer pastures and partly shorter migration routes in the West, the nomad population has a more secure subsistence and is able to concentrate in larger numbers. Villages in the area, on the other hand, are poorer, and administrative control was until recently very defective. The balance

---

[1] e. g. on their past behaviour in situations of conflict and war (Sykes 1921, II: 510-14, Schultze-Holthus, Ch. 6 ff.), and from my own interviews with various Qashqai chiefs and commoners on the subject of hierarchical differences within the tribe.

of power is therefore far more in favour of the nomads; property, crops, and even landed titles are far less secure than in the central areas of Fars. Land purchase and sedentarization thus become far less attractive, and the very economic considerations which encourage that course in the Basseri areas militate against it in the areas under Qashqai control. In the greater complexity of the Qashqai political hierarchy one may thus recognize the effects of many of the same processes as in the simpler autocracy of the Basseri; and considerable differences in organization may thus be derived from relatively subtle differences in the underlying determinants.

In Kerman, on the other hand, strong centralized chiefship is absent, though there is no reason to assume the camp organization of the nomads in that area to be different from that of the Basseri. However, other differences are undeniable. While oasis agriculture continues to be relatively profitable, the area is marginal in terms of the bases it offers for pastoral nomadism. The almost imposed nature of chieftaincy in the Khamseh-Basseri organization (cf. pp. 89-90) is relevant to this. The power of the chief is based mainly on sources outside the tribal system, and does not arise in or become delegated from the scattered nomadic camps. The chief can impose his authority on the Basseri, and be of use to them, because their environment is still so rich as to permit considerable concentration and highly regular movements in the *il-rah*. In the poorer pasture areas to the east, these conditions do not obtain. The density of population must be much lower, and the movements of camps are more erratic, since success in herding depends on the utilization of irregular occurrences of grass and water. The control of such a population is much more difficult, and for the herdsmen themselves such control implies a restriction on their adaptability, rather than a guarantee of their pasture rights. Furthermore, the rewards of chieftaincy are fewer in a poorer environment, so the incentive to invade that status, as did the Ghavam family of Shiraz, is lacking. The possibility for a chief to establish and maintain himself successfully in the dual role of autocratic nomad leader, and respected member of the sedentary *élite*, is thus severely reduced.

The tract of land utilized by the Basseri would seem to lie close to the limits of the area in which centralized nomadic organizations of this type can be maintained. Among the Arab tribes east of them, the extent of centralization appears to have fluctuated considerably;

and with the dissolution of the Khamseh confederacy those groups formerly under central control by Shaibani and Jabbare shaikhs have broken apart, even though the groups have continued a nomadic life.

A further and related factor in centralization and the maintenance of confederacies appears to be trade. There are suggestions that the existence of trade routes through the areas occupied by a nomadic tribe tends to correlate with the degree of centralization in that tribe. This might be expected, since such trade increases the number and importance of contacts with sedentary authorities, and thus the potential external sources of authority which support centralized chiefship. The interests of the Ghavams in the tribes increased the centralization of the nomadic political organizations, and the development of the Khamseh confederacy is thus related to large-scale transit trade through the Gulf ports to Shiraz. The growth in the political importance of the Qashqai confederacy, on the other hand, correlates with the redirection of most English trade through Bushire and the Qashqai area.

Through such centralization and wider interconnections, the nomad tribes become involved in the political dynamics of whole provinces, and at times of the state itself. The development of the Khamseh and Qashqai confederacies in Fars served to polarize the political interest groups in the area into two main factions. In terms of their urban components, these factions have been very unstable; the tribes, on the other hand, have been stable in their alignment in a simple chequerboard pattern. Thus the Khamseh stand against their neighbours the Qashqai; the Mamassani, north of the latter, are aligned with the Khamseh, while the Boir Ahmed, north of them again, align with the Qashqai. Such a chequer-board pattern is clearly related to the border-maintaining effects of inter-tribal hostility (cf. pp. 84 ff.). A forceful chief can impose his authority on camp groups of friendly neighbouring tribes, thereby encroaching on the authority of allied chiefs and even supplanting them. The borders between the maximal political units, or confederacies, can only be maintained if active hostility prevents any exercise of chiefly authority across such borders. A stable alliance between independent units is therefore best established if these units at no point come into territorial contact; and the application of this principle produces a chequer-board pattern.

Finally, the problem of the ethnic diversity among South Persian tribes, and the mechanisms of its persistence, should be discussed. The nomadic Arab population of Fars has according to its own traditions maintained itself without further transplantations of Arabs for more than 1,000 years, while the Turkish populations appear to have arrived in the 12th to 14th centuries. Though living among Persian villages and often subject to Persian administration, in both these groups are found persons and whole sections who know no Persian. Yet there is nothing to suggest any great stability in these populations and their groupings; whole new tribes emerge, while others disappear, as have, e.g., the Lek and allied Lur tribes of most of Fars.

It is important first of all to be clear what the meaning of the ethnic appellations "Arab", "Turk" etc. are. A Western observer will tend to emphasize language as the crucial criterion, and in a very general way will find a correlation between the ethnic name applied to a group, and the language spoken by that group. Local people on the other hand use these same names in referring to tribes as *political* units. I was frequently corrected, e.g. when saying that the Baharlu are Turkish — "Turk" is used as a name for members of the Qashqai confederacy, whereas the Baharlu are members of the Khamseh and therefore "Arab". The frequent confusion in the literature, assigning Arabic language or origin to the Basseri (e.g. Morrier 1837: 232, Field 1939: 216) arises no doubt from this confusion of the political and linguistic reference of the "ethnic" name.

However, ethnic appellations may also be used to refer to origin, or language. Thus, e.g. the Kashkuli are one of the larger tribes of the Qashqai confederacy; they are therefore "Turks" and do in fact also speak Turkish. But they have traditions of being originally Lurs, of one of the old Farsi tribes which used to migrate in the present Basseri channel between Jahrom and Dehbid (cf. also Field 1939: 219, who notes this tradition). It is interesting to note that the Ahl-e-Gholi section of the Basseri has a tradition of origin from the Qarachei, one of the subdivisions of the Kashkuli (cf. p. 52). Historically, the process may have been the reverse, with the Ahl-e-Gholi representing a remnant of the Qarachei in their original locality.

This leads on to the problem of the genesis of tribes and sections — the rate of disappearance of such groups presupposes a certain rate of emergence of new groups. The process of natural growth and segmentation has been discussed; with only imperfect mechanisms for the

131

emergence of internal segments within the recognized units, ordered subdivision by segmentation would seem to require the administrative interference of the chief (pp. 61-68). But since these divisions are at times also in the interest of the chief himself, there is no reason to doubt that they constitute a common pattern for the multiplication and formation of new social groups. In such cases of natural growth and multiplication of units, the new groups will clearly be identified with the same linguistic and ethnic group as was the parental unit.

However, there are clear examples also of a different pattern of growth, which might be characterized as aggregational; and in such cases the question arises of the ethnic classification of the new groups. I have mentioned how the Basseri Darbar shows this aggregational pattern, growing partly by accretion. A group of similiar origin among the Arabs has become an independent tribe. This small tribe (200 tents) under its chief Morteza Khan is known as the *Amaleh;* it became independent in the time of his father's father, Fate Ali Khan. He was simply leader of the camp group surrounding Amir Saleh Khan Shaibani, the central chief of the Shaibani Arabs. Like similar groups elsewhere (the various Amaleh of Arab and Qashqai chiefs, the Darbar of the Basseri, the Arbabdar of the Kurdshuli) this group grew by accretion from outside the tribe as well as within, and became composed of persons of Arab, Farsi, Turkish and Luri origin; their common language was Persian. When Amir Saled Khan died, the political unit around him dissolved, and his Amaleh declared itself independent. Today it is a purely Persian-speaking group, but calls itself, and is called by all, "Arab".

Growth by aggregation presupposes a basic common interest and advantage for members who join the group, in much the same way as kinship affects camp formation within oulads. The most important such common interest of strangers in banding together seems to have been military, and new pastoral nomadic units may develop from simple robber bands. Thus according to Basseri informants, the Qashqai group known as Jam-e-Buzurgi (The Big Gathering) was until a few years ago a small camp group of less than 20 tents. During the war, and later in the period of breakdown of administration under Mossadeq, its members took to banditry, and therefore attracted outsiders so that it has grown by accretion to become an independent oulad of 60 tents.

132

On a larger scale, the whole Kurdshuli tribe has a similar origin[1]. Its nucleus may have been formed by a few camps who broke away from the Qashqai; as an independent unit it is generally credited with an age of no more than 50 years. During the First World War the group was engaged in robbery and did not migrate to the south in the winter (Sykes 1921, II: 481); today it numbers 600-700 tents of pastoral nomads, divided into several sections, each composed of persons of widely varying descent, mainly from different sections of the Qashqai and the Mamassani. In language, most members are bilingual in Turkish and Luri; by others the tribe is usually classified as Turk, sometimes as Lur.

In other words, these aggregational groups are classified ethnically with the political unit with which they are identified, or the ethnic group of origin of their original core. The language spoken by the group may well be different from this. The factors determining the language to be adopted seems to be the language(s) spoken by its constituting members, *and* the contacts which the group maintains. An understanding of the political structure is necessary to evaluate what these contacts are. Since the chief mediates most contacts with sedentary society, the fact that the nomadic population lives dispersed as a minority in a large host population of Persian language and culture is hardly relevant to its linguistic milieu. The institution of centralized chieftainship effectively insulates the tribesmen from contacts with this environment, and establishes them as a centripetally oriented linguistic community, with a few contacts with neighbouring friendly tribes. The persistence of different languages in the same general area is therefore readily understandable; only in cases where aggregational growth patterns produce camps of strongly mixed membership in terms of language does Persian, as the "lingua franca" of the area, become established. Since, however, the ethnic appellations of "Turk", "Lur" etc. mainly refer to tribal, political position, such persistence or change in language does not affect the ethnic classification of the group.

---

[1] Another example of an aggregational origin and predominant growth pattern for a whole tribe was noted above, p. 116, for the tribe founded by Zel-e-Sultan in the Isfahan area.

Appendix I

THE RITUAL LIFE OF
THE BASSERI

Only few references have been made to ritual in this account of the Basseri — hardly any ceremonies have been described, and the behaviour patterns have been discussed in terms of the pragmatic systems of economics, or politics, and hardly ever in terms of their meanings within a ritual system. This has followed from the nature of the material itself, and is not merely a reflection of the present field worker's interests or the analytic orientation of this particular study. The Basseri show a poverty of ritual activities which is quite striking in the field situation; what they have of ceremonies, avoidance customs, and beliefs seem to influence, or be expressed in, very few of their actions. What is more, the different elements of ritual do not seem closely connected or interrelated in a wider system of meanings; they give the impression of occurring without reference to each other, or to important features of the social structure. Perhaps for this reason, I have been unable to integrate many of my observations on ritual practices into the preceding description; and to make the descriptive picture of the Basseri more complete, and in a sense to correct the impression of ritual poverty, I shall therefore present these observations in the following appendix. It concludes with a brief discussion of the reasons for this apparent poverty in ritual idioms, and of the concept of ritual itself.

The Basseri, as Shiah Moslems, accept the general premises and proscriptions of Islam to the extent that they are familiar with them. On the other hand, they are aware of their own laxity in these matters, and are generally uninterested in religion as preached by Persian mullahs, and indifferent to metaphysical problems. The Il-e-Khas, who recently rejoined the tribe after having resided in the Isfahan area for

135

100 years, are a partial exception to this rule, and are today criticized and somewhat despised by other Basseri as being rigidly orthodox, miserly, and humourless.

There are no ritual officers of any kind in the tribe; but in some situations, mainly marriages, the Basseri call in a village mullah or other holy man to perform religious acts. The tribe is also visited by persons claiming sacred status, either as a *Sayyid* — Descendant of the Prophet — or as a *Darvesh* — an ascetic beggar. The latter sing and chant long song cycles on the death of Ali, while the former more frequently write amulets and promise blessings. Both categories are given small gifts of food and other produce, but are frequently ridiculed and abused even while the gifts are given. Everyone I spoke to, including the Sayyids and Darveshes, agreed, however, that this was a recent trend, and that up to 15 years ago people were consistently respectful, and to a great extent really fearful, particularly of the Sayyids. But even then, no members of the tribe were either Sayyids or Darveshes, nor did any such persons reside permanently with the tribe. Within the limits defined by the general tenets of Islam, the Basseri are thus free to develop and elaborate their ceremonies and customs as an autonomous folk system. In the following, these are grouped in terms of their relevance to (I) the yearly cycle, (II) the life cycle, and (III) special practices and avoidances.

(I) The Basseri operate in a sense within three separate calendrical systems: the Islamic year, the Persian or solar year, and the yearly cycle of their own migrations, which brings them past the same series of localities in a regular succession. Each of these cycles is marked by a few ceremonies[1].

There is much confusion among the Basseri with respect to the divisions and events of the Moslem year, though they are continually being reminded of them through their contacts with sedentary society; and even where they have the knowledge, there is great laxness in observing the prescribed customs. The nomads pray irregularly and always individually; even on Friday there is no communal gathering of worshippers within a camp or even within a tent. Islamic feast days are rarely celebrated, though a pious respect for them is often ex-

---

[1] Only the period of March-June, or from the eighth to the eleventh Moslem month, were observed in the field; for the rest of the year I have only general and specific statements by informants.

pressed when decisions on migration schedule are being made (cf. p. 45). Even the fast of Ramadan and the feast of Moharram, of central importance to the surrounding Moslems, are observed and celebrated by few. Thus when we visited the market town of Jahron during Ramadan, the group of nomads I was with went to great trouble to get in by a back door to a shut restaurant and be served a meal, claiming dispensation from fast because we were travelling — which we were not that day. On the other hand, the Moslem calendar is thought to be important in questions of good and bad luck — thus the nomads will not divide a herd on a Friday, nor shear the sheep on a Moslem holiday.

The Persian, or solar, year is of greater importance to the Basseri, since it is in terms of it that the chief organizes and directs the migrations, and it defines the one universally observed feast day: that of *Nowruz*, the Persian New Year, at spring equinox. On this day everyone wears new clothes, or at least an item of new clothing; the women and girls colour their hair and hands with henna; friends and acquaintances greet each other formally, exchanging good wishes for the coming year; and there is much intervisiting and serving of food and tea in the tents of a camp, and between related and adjacent camps, and nomads and village friends. Nowruz falls at the beginning of the main spring migration and therefore marks the beginning of a new year in a very real sense. None the less, the celebrations are not elaborate and time-consuming enough to prevent many groups from striking and moving camp also on that day.

Finally, the migrations themselves form a yearly cycle, and it is in terms of them that the average Basseri conceptualizes time and organizes his life (cf. below, p. 148). In the course of such a cycle, the nomad passes by a succession of localities, and many points along the way are marked with shrines (Imamzadeh/Ziarat) in the form of the graves of holy men. Few of these have any great significance to the nomads, but they usually pray or show respect as they pass by, though they often have no name, and rarely any myth about the actions of the Saint who was buried there. Nor do any of these shrines serve as centres around which larger groups congregate. Individuals may seek such shrines for prayers and special requests for help and support from the dead Saint; in the southern areas of winter dispersal are several shrines which are visited by nomads and villagers alike. A particularly famous and important shrine is that of Said Mohammed, located in the Kurdshuli summer pasture areas. It lies where three very large natural springs burst forth from the foot of the mountain, and is unique in being visited by larger groups of people, rather than separate individuals. Most of the camp groups which regularly pass close to the shrine make a practice of stopping over one day to visit it; men women and children dress in their best clothes and go there together, often several persons from each tent. Each household which is represented should give an animal in sacrifice by the shrine — though often several tents combine for a single sacrifice, to save animals. When the animals have been slaughtered and while they are being cooked, most of the visitors enter the shrine itself, first all the women, then the men, though many remain outside. After this, those who have combined in a sacrifice join in a meal of meat and rice, and members of the same camp group mix while drinking tea. Similar groups of visitors from other camps, on the other hand, are ignored, whereas beggars and shrinekeepers who reside in a small village beside the shrine are given a share of the sacrifice and the cooked rice. Throughout, there is a general lack of ceremonial, and a gay and carefree feeling of a festive picnic prevails.

(II) Rituals connected with the life cycle are considerably more elaborated, and relate mainly to birth, marriage, and death.

Whereas pregnancy is associated with no particular rituals, birth is marked, especially in the case of the first child or the first son, by *khushhali* — happiness expressed by the giving of sweets, and shooting rifles into the air. Every day for the first three days of its life, and every subsequent Wednesday *(Charshambe)* for 40 days, the infant is cut on nose, neck and chest with razor blades, later also on the ears. This is to prevent the child's blood from becoming unclean later in life — a condition revealed by pimples in adolescence. Laceration in front of the ear and on the ear-lobes is also used later in childhood as a remedy against ear-ache.

Boys are circumcised, generally by a village barber or physician, before the age of two months. If circumstances prevent it being done so early, the parents generally wait till the boy is 6-7 years old, since otherwise he is very afraid when the operation is performed. There is no corresponding operation on girls, and no external mark to indicate maturity in either sex.

138

Usually around her 14th year, a girl will start being interested in boys, and may find a sweetheart whom she will meet and kiss in secret trysts. If they are surprised in this, her father will beat her; even when uninterrupted, such relations rarely develop into full-fledged liaisons. These relations have little relevance to future betrothals. In general, sexual abstention is the pattern for boys as well as for girls, in the case of the former perhaps largely because of the lack of opportunities in a small community largely composed of kin, where the girls are required to be virgins at marriage and strictly faithful to their husbands. Even elopements appear to be very rare, and such action was the cause of one of the two cases of homicide within the tribe which I was able to collect.

In the normal course of events, girls are betrothed some time after the age of 15, though not infrequently much later. The men are generally older, and may not be betrothed till the age of 30. Parents may make a promise long before the age appropriate for betrothal, but many prefer to remain uncommitted. The choice of spouse lies squarely in the hands of the parents; and even adult men, e.g. widowers, never negotiate their own marriages, but act through a senior relative.

Once a father and son have agreed to seek a betrothal, the son starts performing a sort of informal bride-service, helping his prospective father-in-law by fetching wood, serving tea, and assisting in tasks requiring the co-operation of several men, such as breaking in young horses for riding, or shearing sheep. Gifts for the girl are also offered to her father, the acceptance of which places him under a certain obligation, while the refusal or return of such gifts is a clear idiom of dismissal.

Finally, if a formal promise can be extracted from the girl's father, this is solemnized the next day in a betrothal ceremony (*aghd-bandun* = the tying of the contract). The crucial feature of this is the drawing up of a marriage contract, usually by a Sayyid or a mullah from a village. This document stipulates the size of the *mahr*, or deferred dowry, but not of the bride-price. The sum of the *mahr* is arrived at by bargaining in which a number of persons participate, and it ranges from 500-1,000 Tomans. The betrothal ceremony consists of a simple feast of rice and meat, given by the boy's father, to which the members of the camp are invited, and in which they partake after witnessing the document. The female guests bring presents of cloth to the future

139

bride, taking care to arrive in a group to create the maximal effect. In a technical legal sense, it is the witnessed document of this betrothal ceremony that constitutes the legal Moslem marriage, the consummation of which is merely deferred.

The wedding itself *(arosi)* follows as soon as the necessary equipment for the future family has been collected and produced, and agreement has been reached on the bride-price, which usually has a value of c. 1,000 Tomans, and is paid partly in sheep, which the girl's father is expected in time to pass on to the young couple. A token gift of sugar is also presented to the bride's senior mother's brother by the groom. The wedding ceremony consists of a great feast, the central features of which are the conducting of the bride from her tent to her husband's tent, the joining of their hands by a person of authority, and the consummation of the marriage.

The whole feast, however, is considerably elaborated, and persons from neighbouring camps, as well as from the camp or camps of the spouses, participate. The feast is given by the groom's parents, who hoist a green or red flag on their tentpole, erect a separate kitchen tent *(ashpaz-khune)* and preferably also a guest tent where they serve food and tea and cigarettes throughout the day. There is music where possible — professional musicians must be brought out from the villages — otherwise dancing by women to rhythmic handclaps, and stick-fights and horse-racing by the men. Guests are greeted by the women of the camp with a high trilling call, used otherwise only for distinguished visitors; everyone who can do so comes to the feast on horse-back, and people all dress in their best clothes.

The bride sits in seclusion in her tent with her female relatives, who help wash her, oiling and combing her head hair and removing body hair, colouring her palms and feet with henna, etc. Meanwhile, a very provisional tent is made by the groom's relatives, under the direction of a man who serves as "barber". It may consist of nothing more than a few gaily coloured blankets thrown over two churning tripods outside the groom's tent; this he enters, and there he is supplied with hot water for washing, and shaving of armpits and pubes. While he washes, his female relatives stand outside the tent, clapping their hands and chanting rhymes: "My brother is going to the bath to become sweet" — "Tie my brother's horse well away from his bath, for in it is a deep deep well, and the horse might break its leg" — "Lowlands

140

in winter, high mountains in summer; lowlands and mountains are good places for marriage". When the groom is clean, he emerges in his pyjamas and puts on new clothes which the barber has laid out for him on a rug outside; while he bathes and dresses, raisins (for blessing) and salt (against evil eye) are flung over him, the bath tent, and the spectators. When he is partly dressed, his face is shaved and his hair cut by the barber.

Male relatives of the groom thereupon erect a small nuptial tent, which he is then taken to inspect. When the word is received that the bride is ready, a group of men from the groom's family ride away to fetch her, bringing a spare horse for her to ride on, while the groom enters the nuptial tent and waits there. When the procession arrives at the girl's tent, her mother and father claim their *ru-aghdi* (on-the-wedding-contract) of 20-30 Tomans, and their *ba-ruzi* (for-the-day) of rice, sugar, and leg of lamb for a feast meal. Bride and bedding are then loaded on the free horse, and covered with a veil. Her father leads her horse, often holding a mirror behind its head, for luck and against evil eye. Dancing women and galloping men accompany and circle the procession. On reaching the vicinity of the nuptial tent, the bride's father generally stops and has to be coaxed on; when he comes close, the groom emerges from the tent, at which point the men try to catch him and beat him. Once he escapes back into the tent, he may come out again unmolested — the horse is brought to the tent opening and the groom emerges to lift the bride down. At this point her father intervenes again, claiming his *pa-ranjun* (foot-hand-journey, for bringing the bride), which he is then promised, usually in the form of an appropriate beast, such as a camel. The groom then lifts the bride down from her horse and carries her into the tent, at which point all the women enter and thereby drive him out, whereupon he stands around rather sheepishly, not participating in the festivities, or retreats from the camp.

At sunset he re-enters the nuptial tent, where his and the bride's hands are joined by a Sayyid, or a prominent man of the community, and then they are left. The only equipment in the tent is the bride's bedding and a clean white cloth for sleeping on, and perhaps some sweets or fruit for a breakfast. A male relative of the groom stands guard outside the tent; when the marriage has been consummated he shoots a gun into the air, and the women of the camp greet the news with their high-pitched trilling. Next morning the white sheet is inspected by both families together; if the girl was not a virgin, her husband may divorce her without giving her the *mahr* dowry and may even, if his family is strong, succeed in getting back the bride-price. The couple sleep in the nuptial tent for three nights; after that they usually reside in the groom's father's tent for a while before they establish an independent household.

Married status is often, though not always, marked by women by a change of hair style, whereby the hair is cut short and bobbed, instead of leaving it long and loosely tucked under the headcloth, in the fashion of unmarried girls. The use of eye make-up is also limited to married women.

According to Basseri informants, the wedding ceremony has changed its form somewhat during the last generation. It used to be that the groom himself went, with his relatives, to fetch the bride; he would help her up on her horse, then mount another horse and set off at full gallop across the plain, pursued by the men, both of his own and his bride's group. If they succeeded in catching him, they would all beat him. This has now been replaced by the smaller show of hostility and sexual jealousy when the groom emerges from the nuptial tent to meet the bride.

Even this milder form of ritual hostility is according to the Basseri now on the decline, and is replaced by a custom borrowed from the villages and towns, which I also saw in one of the Basseri weddings I witnessed.

According to it, the groom comes out of the nuptial tent unmolested, and meets his bride 100-200 meters away from the tent. He there lifts her off her horse and presents her with an orange, which she clasps in her hands and carries to the tent. People say an orange is used because it is a sweet thing, a good thing between friends; some interpret is as a pledge of good treatment, "like an oath on the Koran".

In comparison, death and burial are relatively little elaborated. The persons in the tent where a death has occurred spend the subsequent hours wailing and singing laments, joined at times by male and especially female visitors from other tents of the camp. The corpse is buried within a day of death; for this purpose it is always carried to a village cemetery, never buried out in the hills; prominent men are sometimes brought to the closest shrine for burial. The group within which the

142

death has taken place always remains camped for a day or two to complete the funeral.

The body is washed by a close relative of the same sex, and laid out in orthodox Moslem fashion. No ritual specialist from the village is present; a group of male relatives, though usually not those most closely related to the dead person, such as parents or children, perform the whole ceremony alone. Since knowledge of the Koranic specifications for burial is incomplete, the digging and construction of the slab coffin, and the arrangement of the body in it, take much thought. A literate or quasi-literate person tries to chant the appropriate texts from the Koran, while after the corpse is laid into the grave, one man sits at the head of the grave holding a stick which touches the dead person's head, to maintain contact with him until all the earth is thrown over the grave. A slab of stone is erected at the head and one at the foot of the grave, and the piled earth is decorated with dry grass and weeds and the short thorny brush which grows on the sun-drenched hills of the cemetery, pathetically referred to by the bereaved as *gwul* — "flowers". Throughout, there is no great show of sorrow, only a quiet and serious attempt at doing everything properly.

The following evening or night, the women and closest male relatives go to the grave, light fires at its head and foot, weep and wail, and finally distribute sweets. Three days and seven days after the death, feasts should be given in honour of the dead by the relatives, even though they have probably moved on by then to new camp-sites; if the deceased was a prominent man, people from other camps throughout the tribe may come for these feasts, bringing gifts such as lambs. Exceptional love for the dead person is expressed by regular distributions of sweets every Friday for a period of time, sometimes even for several years.

Later on, the graves of close relatives are occasionally visited when the camp group passes through the neighbourhood. In cases where the death was considered particularly tragic, small groups of mourners may assemble for a visit to the grave every year; particularly the women maintain this practice. The group will approach the grave weeping and crying "Oh Mother, Oh Father, Oh Beloved!", and then sit around the grave crying and chanting laments. Often, they will knock at the stone slabs of the grave with pebbles, to call the attention

143

of the dead to their laments; before leaving, they distribute sweets to the village children, who shamelessly congregate there to benefit from the pickings. Improvised laments are also chanted after conversations in the tent about close dead persons, or at other occasions of sorrow and despair — often when a child has been beaten by its parent, he or she will sit a short distance from the tent, wailing and chanting laments.

(III) A certain number of special prescriptions and avoidances are also observed which have no direct relation to the yearly cycle or the life cycle. These are generally associated with notions of good and bad luck, especially with respect to the flocks, and with witchcraft beliefs in the form of beliefs in the evil eye.

Most striking is the taboo on association of important animals in certain situations: thus a horse must not be permitted to approach the sheep while they are being sheared, or milked, while lambs, kids and foals should not enter a tent in which there is new-born infant. Similarly, a man riding a horse, or a man who is very tired, should not approach the tent in which a new-born baby lies, likewise a woman wearing gold or yellow or white beads. In these cases, however, if the person stops a short distance from the tent and the baby is brought out to meet him or her, they can subsequently enter without causing harm.

More diffuse are the beliefs in the evil eye of envy *(nazar* or *cheshm-e-shur),* and in the means of protection against it. Though many people profess complete scepticism, the belief is widespread that evil eye and envious thoughts in any person have certain automatic effects which may at times cause illness and death. Though all people have it, some are much stronger than others, and particularly persons with blue eyes are suspect. Since illness and death are the consequences, only live objects, i. e. animals and children, may be the objects and victims of evil eye.

There is no cure or effective penance for the evil eye, but since its efficacy depends on the spontaneous nature of the envy, a number of simple protective devices may shield the animal or child. All of them are designed to make the spectator immediately aware of his thoughts: a string of blue beads, or rags, broken pottery, or other objects of striking contrast tied around the neck or leg of the animal or child. On the other hand, strong amulets *(taviz* = citations from the Koran)

144

which may be obtained from Sayyids, may protect a person by their inherent power, without the knowledge of the envious spectator.

Again since it is the unconscious envy that harms, only friends, acquaintances and relatives *(khodeman* = one's own people) cast the evil eye, while declared enemies are impotent to do so. The effect of the evil eye may be to cause illness or one or a series of accidents; sometimes children or animals simply wither. In cases where strange behaviour or staring by someone causes suspicion which is confirmed by subsequent disaster (such as in one case I heard of, where the unexplained death of a 3-year-old boy followed within 24 hours of the visit of two men from a different camp to the tent where he lived), general indignation may lead to sanctions within the camp of the suspects, such as severe beating or even lynching.

In connection with joyful events or particular successes, e. g. in hunting, a person is expected to give sweets to the members of his community. This is explained as an effort to prevent envy and evil eye, and to express a feeling of friendship and good will towards all. The reciprocal of this is the habit of associating expressions of admiration with pious exclamations, rendering them incapable of harm, and expressions such as *dun ziat* — may the milk be plentiful — as greetings on approaching persons engaged in milking.

Finally, games and play may be regarded as a form of ritual behaviour. I have mentioned above the group dances by women, and stick-duel dancing by men. Small children also play at rhythmic word-games, chanting ditties to a simple 2 : 4 beat with sticks on the tent-cloth or a hollow object, to words such as: "The flock ran up on top of the mountain / my brother brought it down again." Men play backgammon and a type of whist. The only team game I ever saw was a rather brutal one between two teams of four young boys each, one group attacking, and the other defending four shallow pits according to special rules. Success in the attack gave the winning side the right to whip the defeated team, followed by a reversal of their positions as attackers and defenders. In this, as in cards, much time is taken up by attempts at, and accusations of, cheating.

The ritual idioms described above are largely very naive and simple, and they are not combined in larger complexes to communicate more subtle meanings. The use of sugar and sweets to express amity between persons, and thereby prevent ill-feelings and maintain literally sweetness in social relations; the use of salt and mirrors against evil eye, and of objects in striking contexts to create incongruity and awareness of evaluative thoughts in an observer; the custom of explicit well-wishing in situations where one might have been envious — all these idioms show an obvious association of their ritual meanings, and their characteristics or tangible properties; none of them are derivative from other complexes of meanings and beliefs, and all of them are consistent with the pragmatic and un-ritualistic attitude I have implied in my whole description of Basseri life. The one striking custom that seems to fall outside this pattern is the cutting and bleeding of infants, which incidentally is found also among Lur tribes of Fars. With the lack of elaboration of apparently similar themes, however, it seems methodologically hopeless to speculate on the possible connection of this practice with notions regarding sacrifice and blood, or circumcision. In general, I feel that the above attempt at an exhaustive description of the ceremonies and explicit ritual practices of the Basseri reveals a ritual life of unusual poverty.

To me this raises an inevitable question — can one isolate particular reasons, or explanations, for this apparent poverty? In the present case, I feel that some further analysis of the material may serve to modify, and in a sense correct, this picture.

In the above description, I have adopted a sort of "common sense" view of ritual, and compiled a list of those customs or actions which are explicitly non-technical, essentially those which the Basseri themselves classify in categories translatable as "ceremonies", "religion", and "magic". Greater sophistication in the definition of ritual might lead to an expansion of the field of inquiry.

In the literature of social anthropology, a number of different, but closely related, refinements of ritual and related concepts have been presented. The views expressed in Leach's (1954) discussion seem to me the clearest and most stimulating. In these terms, ritual may be defined as the symbolic aspect of non-verbal actions — those acts or aspects of acts which *say* something, in terms of shared values and meanings, rather than *do* something in terms of predictable material and economic consequences (ibid. pp. 12-13). By isolating the symbolic *aspect* of actions, one avoids the difficulties inherent in Durkheim's absolute distinction between the sacred and the profane (ibid. p. 12).

146

However, the dismissal of an absolute distinction between sacred and profane contexts raises certain problems, revealed in relation to the associated concept of myth. Myth is defined as the counterpart of ritual; myth as a statement in words "says" the same thing as ritual, regarded as a statement in action (ibid pp. 13-14). To this, most anthropologists would agree. But the above definition makes "ritual" of *all* symbolic aspects of acts, whereas no one would hold that all speech, because it has meaning, is "myth". If only because of the presence, apparently in all cultures, of concepts such as ceremony, religion, and magic, we need to be able to distinguish between rituals as systems of communication, and the mere fact that all actions, no matter how pragmatic, have "meanings" to the persons who observe them. Though Durkheim's dichotomy of sacred and profane is untenable, the feeling remains that rituals are actions especially pregnant with meaning, that they are at least in a relative sense set apart from other acts, for one thing because they are, in a sense, more important. Very tentatively, then, one might say that ritual is the symbolic aspect of acts in contexts vested with particular value.

Before returning to the material there is one further point I wish to make. Anthropologists often make the unneccessary and naive assumption that since the symbolic aspect and the technical aspect of actions may be separated by analysis, their correlates in the *form* of an act must also be separable. They seem to argue that technical requirements impose certain restrictions on the form of an act — therefore, its symbolic meanings must lie elsewhere, in those formal features that are technically superfluous or unneccessary. This does not follow. Clearly, there is no reason why the very forms of an act which reflect the technical imperatives may not *also* be vested with central and crucial meaning in a symbolic system or context.

We may now return to the material at hand, and look for further sets of acts, or aspects of acts, which carry and communicate meanings in contexts vested with particular value. It becomes overwhelmingly clear that the whole basic system of activities involved in the economic adaptation of the Basseri, of camping and herding and travelling, are pregnant with such meanings, and that the context in which they take place, that of the great migration, is vested with extreme value.

Let me try to show what this statement implies — firstly, the kinds of meanings of sociological relevance which these actions appear to

147

have, and secondly, the value which is placed on their context, the migration, which warrants their classification with more conventional rituals. Some of the most explicit meanings associated with camping and travelling have been touched on already (pp. 42 ff.). The camp itself, with its semicircle of fires, alone in an empty landscape, and constantly re-pitched in new localities in changing circumstances, serves as a clear expression of the social unity of the group which inhabits it, and of the mechanisms whereby that group is maintained. The caravan which travels the long way over steppes and through valleys and across passes cannot but become a procession: those at the head lead the way, they must decide which path to take, while those behind can have no active part in that decision; the aggregation in a camel and donkey train and the dispersal over a restricted plain for camping repeat daily the social facts of group allegiance and divisions; the sullen hostility of unfamiliar spectators wherever the caravan road goes through a village marks the caravan off as a group totally different from the sedentary communities. Finally, the scatter sometimes of a thousand tents over a single valley floor rich in pastures, the parallel movement over a plain of scores of caravans, visible as low lingering clouds of dust on the horizon — such occasions serve to dramatize the community of membership in tribe and confederacy, and their segmental structure.

These meanings, or symbolic aspects, of the activities are of the same logical order and partly of the same form as many of the ritual idioms of a religious ceremony, as these have been analysed by anthropologists elsewhere. But they can only be compared to these if the context in which they take place is one of correspondingly predominant value. The context of these meanings is the cycle of migrations, which dominates the life and organizes most of the activities of the Basseri.

It is an economic necessity for the Basseri to move with their flocks in each season to where pastures can be found. But the migration has a value to them exceeding even this, as is apparent from the following considerations. Firstly, time and space alike are interpreted with reference to migration. Thus (as noted elsewhere, Barth 1960), when we passed through the Sarvestan valley in the beginning of April, the nomads collected a great supply of truffles which enlivened our diet for a week. When I asked them whether truffles appear only

148

briefly in the beginning of April, or perhaps are found only in the Sarvestan valley, the only answer I could obtain was "yes". My two alternatives were to them merely two ways of expressing the same experience: a season is a stretch of country, and *vice versa* — or rather, both are aspects of a unit within the migration cycle.

Other types of data also show the value placed on the migration itself. When internal Persian administration collapsed in 1941 the sanctions behind forced sedentarization were removed. All the Basseri expressed their reaction as one of resuming migrations — not as "becoming pastoralists again". As a matter of fact, most of them had very few animals, and some appear to have resumed migration entirely without stock — the supreme value to them lay in the freedom to migrate, not in the circumstances that make it economically advantageous.

Finally, if this is so, if the migration is a context vested by the Basseri with particularly great value, this should also be revealed in the emotional engagement of those who participate in it. The long journey of a great number of flocks and people from the low plains to the high mountains is in itself a highly dramatic set of events. utilized e. g. in Cooper and Shodesack's book (1925) and film on the migrations of the Bakhtiari. If one can show that the Basseri react significantly to the inherent dramatic structure of their migrations, this is a measure of the value which they place on it as a context for activities.

When I joined the Darbar tent group, it was slowly moving from the broken mountains south of Harm towards the large plain of Mansurabad, which serves as an area of congregation before the large spring migration starts. The feeling of general excitement, the richness of "meaning" in the technical acts of coming under way and approaching this goal that is only a stage of a longer journey, was a strong subjective experience. In an attempt to devise a less subjective measure of this noticeable tension, excitement, or emotional involvement, I subsequently recorded the times of awakening, packing, and departure of the camp. The assumption was that, apart from the interference caused by random factors and changing natural obstacles, these times would reflect changes in the level of excitement or tension. and thus register the extent of the nomad's perception of, and subjective participation in, the migration as a drama, as an ordered

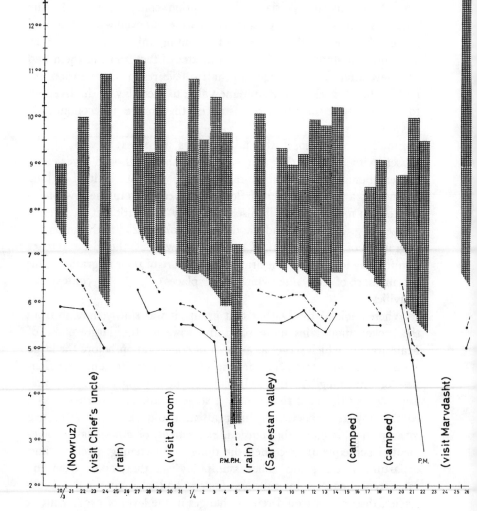

Fig. 9. Time-chart for the Darbar camp's spring migration in 1958. Abscissa: calendar dates; ordinate: hours of the day. For each day of migration, the following are indicated: the time of striking tents in the morning, the time when starting to load the donkeys, the times of departure from the camp site (with span of time between first and last households to depart), and the time of

150

arrival at new camp site. The duration of each daily migration is thus indicated by the cross-hatched column. Lines have been drawn connecting the times of striking the tents (solid) and times of loading (stippled) on the consecutive days of each migratory cycle, showing the cyclical trend towards progressively earlier rising and departure.

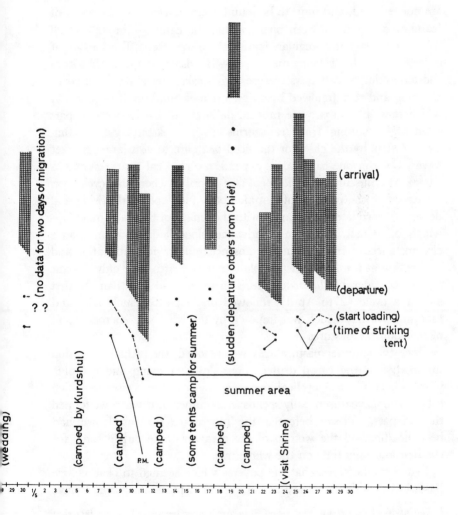

and unique context. Rising tensions should be expressed in earlier awakening, more rapid packing, and earlier departures; a lack of reaction and involvement should give no, or random, variations in these times.

The resulting data are presented in Fig. 9. In spite of the multitude of disturbing variables — such as the fact that the beasts of burden are not tethered, and have to be found every morning, or the event of feasts or accidents or even births within the camp — in spite of all this, some clear and regular features are revealed. Tension — if indeed this is what is being measured — builds up progressively within shorter cycles of 3-6 days, before it is broken by a day or two of camping and rest, followed by a new cycle of build-up. The points at which these build-ups were broken, defining the cycles, were in part accidental, resulting from rainstorms, in part arbitrary, reflecting direct orders by the chief, or the need or desire to visit larger market towns. Only in one case did it depend on physical features and a climax of muscular exertion (5th of April), when the cycle was broken after the crossing of a major pass. Nor does early rising and departure correlate significantly with the length of the daily march — which is, in fact, unknown in advance, since it depends on chance circumstances of crop presence or absence and previous utilization and occupation at a number of possible alternative sites. The only deviant case of considerably *later* departure on the second day than the first day of a cycle (27th April), followed one such extremely long and fatiguing journey which was imposed by the wholesale encroachment of fields on the pastures[1].

Once the summer pasture area was reached, the feeling of tension subsided, and the camp drifted more slowly, moving and camping without any marked cyclical patterns, towards the region in which that particular camp usually spends the summer. But when we topped the last pass, and saw before us the mountains for which we had been heading, all the women of the caravan broke out in song, for the first and only time on the whole trip.

I suggest, therefore, that the poverty which seemed to characterize Basseri ritual life is an artifact of the descriptive categories I have

---

[1] The atypical curves for the period 7-14 April may be related to the fact that the group during this period passed *by* the town of Shiraz, at a distance, searching for a campsite where they could wait while I made a brief visit to Shiraz.

employed, and that it depends essentially on the naive assumption that *because* certain activities are of fundamental practical economic importance, they cannot *also* be vested with supreme ritual value. If one grants this possibility, on the other hand, it becomes very reasonable to expect the activities connected with migration to have a number of meanings to the nomads, and to be vested with value to the extent of making the whole migration the central rite of nomadic society. It is, admittedly, a methodological problem to demonstrate the value that is placed on migration, when this value is not, in fact, expressed by means of technically unnecessary symbolic acts and exotic paraphernalia. I have tried briefly to show that this value is revealed in the way the migration cycle is used as a primary schema for the conceptualization of time and space, in the fact that many nomads, after the external disturbance of enforced sedentarization, resumed migratory life in spite of economic costs, and finally, in the emotional engagement of the participants in the migration. The latter data show that the participants respond, not to the utilitarian aspects of the activities — to good pastures and potential butter-fat — but to the movement and its dramatic form — to the *meanings* implicit in the sequence of activities.

This realization is important for the understanding of Basseri life — by it, the description contained in the preceding chapters is transformed from an external and objective description of the economic and social arrangements within a tribe to a description of central features of the culture of that tribe, the meanings and values which make up their life. Whereas this is usually achieved by an exploration of religious and ceremonial practices, in which these meanings and values are predominantly expressed, this could not, because of the nature of the material, be done here. The Basseri differ from many people in that they seem to vest their central values in, and express them through, the very activities most central to their ecologic adaptation. This is perhaps possible for them only because of the peculiar nature of that adaptation — because of the picturesque and dramatic character of the activities, which makes of their migrations an engrossing and satisfying experience.

153

WORKS CITED

Abbott, K. E., 1857: Notes taken on a Journey eastwards from Shiraz. . in 1850. *Journal of the Royal Geographical Society.* Vol. 27 pp. 149-85. London

Barth, F., 1953: *Principles of Social Organization in Southern Kurdistan* Universitetets Etnografiske Museum Bulletin No. 7. Oslo.
⎯1959: *Political Leadership among Swat Pathans.* London School of Economics Monographs on Social Anthropology No. 19. London
1960: The land use patterns of migratory tribes of South Persia. *Norsk Geografisk Tidsskrift*

⎯ Cooper, M. G. 1925: *Grass* G. P. Putman's Sons, New York.

Curzon, G. N., 1892: *Persia and the Persian Question.* 2 vols.

Dames, M. L., 1902: Note on Major Syke's Gypsy vocabulary. *Journal of the Anthropological Institute* vol. 32 pp. 350-52. London.

Demorgny, G., 1913: Les reformes administratives en Perse: Les tribus du Fars. *Revue du Monde Musulman* vol. 22 pp. 85-150. Paris.

Field, H., 1939: *Contributions to the Anthropology of Iran.* Anthropological Series, Field Museum of Natural History vol. 29 No. 1. Chicago.

Furnival, J. S., 1944: *Netherlands India — a study of plural economy.* Cambridge University Press.

Homans, G. C., 1950: *The Human Group.* Harcourt, Brace & Co. New York.

Lambton, A. K. S., 1953: *Landlord and Peasant in Persia.* Oxford University Press. London.

Leach, E. R., 1954: *Political Systems of Highland Burma.* G. Bell & Sons Ltd. London.

Monteith, W., 1857: Notes on the Routes from Bushire to Shiraz. *Journal of the Royal Geographical Society* vol. 27 pp. 108-19.

Morier, J., 1837: Some Account of the I'liyáts, or Wandering Tribes of Persia. *Journal of the Royal Geographical Society* vol. 7 pp. 230-42.

Radcliffe-Brown, A. R., 1924: The Mother's brother in South Africa. Reprinted in: *Structure and Function in Primitive Society.* Cohen & West, London 1952.

Rich, C. J., 1836: *Narrative of a Residence in Koordistan . . . . and an account of a visit to Shirauz and Persepolis.* 2 vol.s James Duncan, London.

Schulze-Holthus, 1954: *Daybreak in Iran.* Staples Press Ltd. London.

Stenning, D. J., 1958: Household viability among the Pastoral Fulani. in: J. Goody ed.: *The Developmental Cycle in Domestic Groups.* Cambridge Papers in Social Anthropology No. 1.

Sykes, Sir P., 1902: Anthropological notes on Southern Persia. *Journal of the Anthropological Institute* vol. 32 pp. 339-49. London.
1906: The Gypsies of Persia. *Journal of the Anthropological Institute* vol. 36 pp. 302-11. London.
1921: *A History of Persia* 2 vols. IInd ed. Macmillan & Co. London.

INDEX

Abbott, 120
Abdul Yusufi *taife,* 52
Abduli section, 51 f., 86
Agha Jan Beg, 116
aghd - e-nume, see Marriage contract
agriculture, 4, 9, 105
Ahl-e-Gholi section, 51 f., 131
Ahmad, 64
Ainalu tribe, 3, 86, 119
Ali Akbar, 87
Ali Ghambari section, 51, 72, 86
Ali Marduni oulad, 51, 56, 60
Ali Mirzai, 52, 72, 85, 117 f.
Ali Shah Gholi section 51 f., 68, 72
Amaleh 128, 132
Amir Saleh Khan, 132
amulets, 136, 144
animal products, 7 f.
animals, domesticated, 6 f., 13
Arabs, 2, 50, 52, 86, 116, 127, 129 ff.
army: administration, 26, 67, 96
Avaz Agha Farhadpur, 60
avoidances, 144 ff.

Baharlu tribe, 2 f., 86, 119, 131
Bala Velayati oulad, 51 f.
Band Amir, 5, 116
Bandar Abbas, 87
ba-ruzi, 141
Basseri: early sources on, 3;
    genetic connections of, 2;
    group definition, 1.

bazaar, 92, 98
Benarou-Mansurabad plain, 5
betrothal, 139
bilingualism, 1 f., 133
birth control, 114
birth rate, 114, 118 f., 125
birth rituals, 138
Boir Ahmed, 2, 130
bride-price, 18 f., 140
bride-service, 139
Bugard Basseri, 2
butter, 8, 17

Calendrical system, 136 ff.
camel, 6 f.
camp: changes in membership, 65;
    composition of, 39, 127;
    endogamy, 35 f., 39 ff.;
    external relations, 39, 46 f.;
    incorporation of new members,
      38, 47;
    increasing agnatic homogene-
      ity, 62, 65 f.;
    lack of segmentation, 41 ff.;
    leadership, 26 f., 81;
    primary community, 25 f., 35,
      93, 43 ff., 58 f., 81, 127;
    recruitment to, 26, 59;
    techniques of decision-making,
      43 ff.;
    versus oulad, 60 ff.;

Ghorbati: 91 f.;
     camps, 91;
     crafts, 92 f.
     migratory cycle, 92;
     pariah group, 92
goats, 6, 13
grazing rights, see pastures
Gypsy, 8, 91 f.

Habibullah Ghavam-ul-Mulk, 88
habitat, 3
Haji Ibrahim, 87
Haji Kohzad, 59
Haji Mohammed Khan, 72, 86, 115
Hanai section, 51 f., 68
Hassan Ali Khan, 83
headman, 26, 55
herd, care of, 102 f.;
     checks on growth, 126;
     ownership, 13, 16 ff., 123 f.;
     rate of growth, 103
herding: 6f;
     co-operative units, 21 ff., 42;
     harbouring, 13 f., 103;
     losses of animals, 7, 102 f.;
     theft, 47
hides, 7 f.
historical tradition, 2 f., 52
history, 3, 85 ff., 131
holy men, 32, 136 f.
horse, 6
hospitality, 94, 102
hostilities: between tribes, 94 f., 130
household: 11 ff.
     authority of women, 34;
     labour division, 15 f., 20 f.;
     maintenance and replace-
        ment of, 18 ff.;
     organization, 14 f.
household equipment, 13
hunting, 9
Husein Ahmedi, 52
hygiene, 114 f., 120

Ibrahim Khan, 88
Il, 50

Il-e-Khas section, 50 ff., 55, 73, 116,
     135
il-rah, see migration route
immigration, 116, 118
inheritance: 20;
     anticipatory, 19 f., 34, 39,
        106 f.;
     conflicts over, 20;
     of daughters, 20
irrigation, 4
Isfahan area, 2, 52, 92, 116, 135
Islam, 135 f.

Jabbare, dynasty, 86
Jahrom, 5, 98, 131
Jam-e-Buzurgi, 132
Jouchin section, 51, 56, 76

Kalantar, 72
Karim Khan Zand, 87, 119
kashk, 8
Kashkuli tribe, 131
katkhoda, 26, 55, 105
Kerman, 116, 127, 129
Khamseh confederacy, 1 f., 86, 88 f.,
     93, 130 f.
Khan, 72
Khavanin, 74
Khorasan, 52
khune, 11
khushhali, 138
kinship: affinal relations, 32 ff.;
     agnatic, 29 ff.;
     bilateral, 41;
     matrilateral, 32, 34, 60;
     patrilineal descent, 30, 55
Kolumbei section, 51, 60, 72 f.
Korejei oulad, 51 f.
Kowli, 91
Kuh-i-Bul, 1, 6
Kur river, 5
Kurdshuli tribe, 2, 94, 133

Labour, division of: 15 f., 101 f.
Labu Musa section, 51, 60, 86
Lak lurs, 119

157

158

ritual: analysis of, 146 f.;
     poverty in idioms, 135, 146,
     150 f.
riz safid, 26
ru-aghdi, 141

sacrifice, 138
Salvestuni section, 51 f.
Sarvestan valley, 148
Sarvestan village, 52
Sayyid, 136, 145
section: 50 ff., 68;
     coalescing process, 68 f.;
     genetic relations, 52 f.;
     list of names, 51;
     subdivisions of, 50 ff.
sedentarization, 3, 65 f., 106 ff., 116 ff.,
     125 ff.
sedentary communities, 97
sedentary market, 97 f.
segmentation, 67, 132
Semirun, 2
Semnan, 2
servant, 21
settled populations, 4
sexual abstention, 139
Shahbani oulad, 51, 64
Shahryar, 60
Shaibani Khans, 86, 132
sheep: 6, 13
     economic returns, 99
shepherds: 6, 15 f., 18, 22;
     hired, 21, 103
Shiraz, 1 f., 4, 96
Shirbahah payment, 33
Shisbeluki, 93
shrines, 137 f.
spinning, 8, 15
Sykes, 87, 119 f.

Taife, see section
Teheran, 92, 96
tenancy, 9, 104 f.
tent, 11 f., 91
tentcloth, 8
teraz contract, 14
tira, see section
topography, 3
trade: 9 f.;
     in bazaar, 98;
     as a factor in centralization,
     130;
     with villagers, 90 f, 108
tribal organization, 50 ff., 54 ff.
tribe: 49 ff.;
     aggregational growth, 132;
     external relations, 78 f., 89 f.,
     93 f.;
     subdivisions of, 50 f.
tribesmen: social position, 109 f.
Turk, 131

Vegetation, 3 f.
villages: purchase of, 95

Water supply, 12, 120
wealth: checks on fluctuations, 108 ff.
weaving, 8, 14
wedding, 140 ff.
Weisi, 52, 62, 72, 119
witchcraft, see evil eye
wool, 7 f.

Yar Mohammed, 63 f.
Yazd-e-Khast, 2
Yazd-Isfahan plain, 2
Yusuf Beg Nafar, 85

Zarghami, 89
Zel-e-Sultan, 1166
Zohrabi section, 51, 68

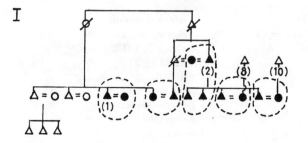

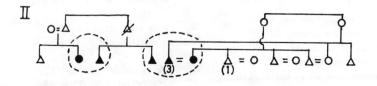

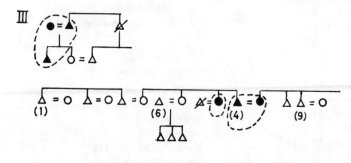

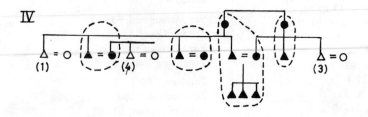

Fig. 10. *Herding units of the Darbar camp. The adult personnel of each household is circled by a stippled line. The persons in each herding unit (I—X) are drawn in black, with their kinship relations to select persons in other herding units of camp indicated. The leading men of the community are identified by Arabic numerals.*

160

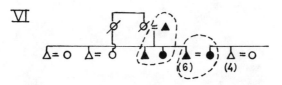

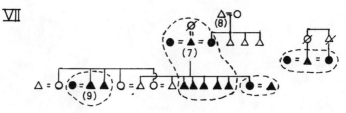

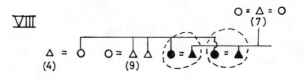

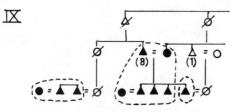

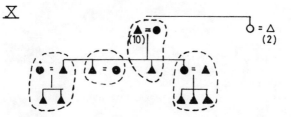

161